STRIKING
GOLD

GOLDEN STATE WARRIORS
NBA CHAMPIONS

Nicky Brillowski, Book and Cover Design

ISBN: 978-1-940056-29-6

Printed in the United States of America
KCI Sports Publishing   3340 Whiting Avenue, Suite 5   Stevens Point, WI 54481
Phone: 1-800-697-3756   Fax: 715-344-2668
www.kcisports.com

CONTENTS

INTRO ===

Let the party begin. The Golden State Warriors are NBA Champions.

For 40 years basketball fans in the Bay Area have been waiting to utter those words. And now it has finally happened.

Strength in Numbers was the Warriors slogan all year and fit this squad perfectly as it took a complete team effort and an incredible display of depth to knock off LeBron James and the Cavaliers in the NBA Finals.

Led by first-year coach Steve Kerr these Warriors were a joy to watch. Moving the ball with precision on offense, the shooting of the Splash Brothers, tenacious defense and the all out hustle displayed night in and night out made this championship team easy to love.

As we began working on this commemorative edition it quickly became evident we could fill three books with all of the highlights the Warriors provided this year. Hopefully, this one book and the moments we've selected will suffice.

We hope you enjoy a look back at a truly remarkable team and season. ■

The members of the Golden State Warriors hold the championship trophy as they celebrate winning the NBA Finals against the Cleveland Cavaliers. *AP Photo | Darron Cummings*

WARRIORS 127 • LAKERS 104

THOMPSON POURS IN 41 AS WARRIORS BEAT LAKERS IN HOME OPENER

Klay Thompson celebrated his big payday with a breakout performance against the player he idolized as a kid growing up in Southern California.

Thompson scored a career-high 41 points in his first game since signing a contract extension, teaming with backcourt star Stephen Curry to carry the Golden State Warriors past Kobe Bryant and the winless Los Angeles Lakers 127-104 on Saturday night.

"I'm not going to lie, it's a great feat," Thompson said. "It's something I'll look back on one day and say, 'That's cool.'"

Thompson, who a day before inked a four-year maximum extension worth about $70 million, shot 14-for-18 from the floor. Curry added 31 points and 10 assists, and the Warriors withstood Bryant's big plays to thrill a blue-shirt-wearing sellout crowd of 19,596 in the team's home opener.

"It was like the rising star at that position going against the guy who's been the best for 15 years," Warriors coach Steve Kerr said. "It was fun to watch."

Bryant scored 19 of his 28 points in the third quarter and nearly brought the depleted Lakers back with one improbable shot after another. Instead, Thompson smothered Bryant in the final quarter – holding him to one point – and Los Angeles lost its fourth game in five nights.

The Lakers are 0-4 for the first time since the 1957-58 season, when the franchise was located in Minneapolis, Minnesota.

Warriors power forward David Lee sat out with a strained left hamstring for the second straight game, which Kerr attributed to another slow start. Unlike the Lakers, though, Golden State could lean on its talented tandem and a deep roster to eclipse Bryant's brilliance.

Jordan Hill finished with 23 points and five rebounds to help the Lakers build a 43-33 lead in the second quarter, a run that silenced the crowd and had Warriors co-owner Joe Lacob sitting in a courtside seat with his hand under his chin staring into the stands in frustration.

That was a familiar look last season when Lacob's team lost several home games to inferior competition, which played a part in Mark Jackson's firing. This time, Kerr called timeout and got his team to respond.

Golden State scored 14 straight points and ended the half leading 61-55 behind a series of scintillating highlights – including a behind-the-back pass from Curry that led to a dunk for Andre Iguodala.

Golden State Warriors' Klay Thompson celebrates past Los Angeles Lakers' Kobe Bryant after scoring during the second half.
AP Photo | Ben Margot

▲Lakers' Kobe Bryant (24) drives the ball between Warriors' Klay Thompson, left, and Andrew Bogut during the second half. *AP Photo | Ben Margot*

◄Lakers' Carlos Boozer (5) lays up a shot past Warriors' Andrew Bogut (12) during the first half. *AP Photo | Ben Margot*

All of Bryant's brilliance, including a twisting layup while getting fouled by Festus Ezeli late in the second quarter, couldn't lead the Lakers to victory. He showed off an array of fadeaways and runners in the third quarter that even left some Warriors fans wowed.

"He was making some crazy shots," Thompson said.

But Golden State's dynamic duo erased anything Bryant did. Thompson made five of seven shots from 3-point range, and Curry finished 10-of-19 shooting, including 3-of-8 from beyond the arc.

"It's tough to stay on top," Thompson said. "They've had their great runs. I think it's the Warriors' turn, man."■

WARRIORS 114 • HEAT 97

CURRY TURNS UP THE HEAT

So much for Stephen Curry's mini-shooting slump.

Curry scored 40 points on 11-of-18 shooting, and the Golden State Warriors beat the Miami Heat 114-97 on Tuesday night for their sixth consecutive victory.

"You just feel a rhythm," said Curry, who was 8-for-24 in his previous two games. "I had guys set some great screens early to kind of get me going. You start finding shots and it feels good. Even the ones I missed terribly felt good, which is pretty funny."

Klay Thompson had 24 points for the Warriors, who shot 57 percent. Curry finished 8-of-11 from 3-point range.

"You always stay confident, stay ready," Curry said. "You win games all sorts of ways with different individual performances. How we shot last game had nothing to do with this game. If we execute our offense well, you're going to get good shots."

Golden State scored 14 straight points to open a 107-95 lead with 2:50 to go. Curry and Thompson capped the run with consecutive 3-pointers.

"The beauty of this team is we can play both ends," Warriors coach Steve Kerr said. "We have the personnel to score. We have the personnel to guard."

Chris Bosh scored 26 points for Miami, and Luol Deng had 16. James Ennis' dunk with 9:11 left was the Heat's last field goal.

"They played their best basketball in the fourth quarter," Heat coach Erik Spoelstra said. "We got caught up in some tough

Warriors forward Draymond Green dunks over Miami Heat forward Shawne Williams, left, and center Chris Bosh, right. *AP Photo | Lynne Sladky*

Warriors guard Stephen Curry (30) shoots over Miami Heat forward Udonis Haslem (40).
AP Photo | Lynne Sladky

possessions. Their defense really stepped up and then they started to score and we just weren't able to sustain from there."

Miami led by 16 in the first half but Golden State closed the second quarter with a 23-8 surge. Draymond Green made two free throws with 9.8 seconds left to cut the Heat's lead to 62-61 at the break.

Golden state carried the momentum over to the second half. Curry hit three 3 pointers in the third period and his two free throws with 58.2 seconds remaining put Golden State head, 89-82.

"This game was a huge challenge for us, probably our biggest challenge defensively we've faced all year because they present a lot of problems," Kerr said. "Second half – everybody was more in tune. We got to their 3-point shooters. We ran them off the line. In the end, we got it rolling."

Harrison Barnes finished with 12 points and Andrew Bogut had 10 rebounds for the Warriors. Bogut started after sustaining a right orbital bone contusion on Sunday.

The Heat got off to a nice start, opening a 31-22 lead on Mario Chalmers' corner 3-pointer with 1:51 left in the first quarter.

"I don't really get what we think or what we do down the stretch against good teams, the elite teams," Bosh said. "For some reason we just forget everything – offense and defense execution."∎

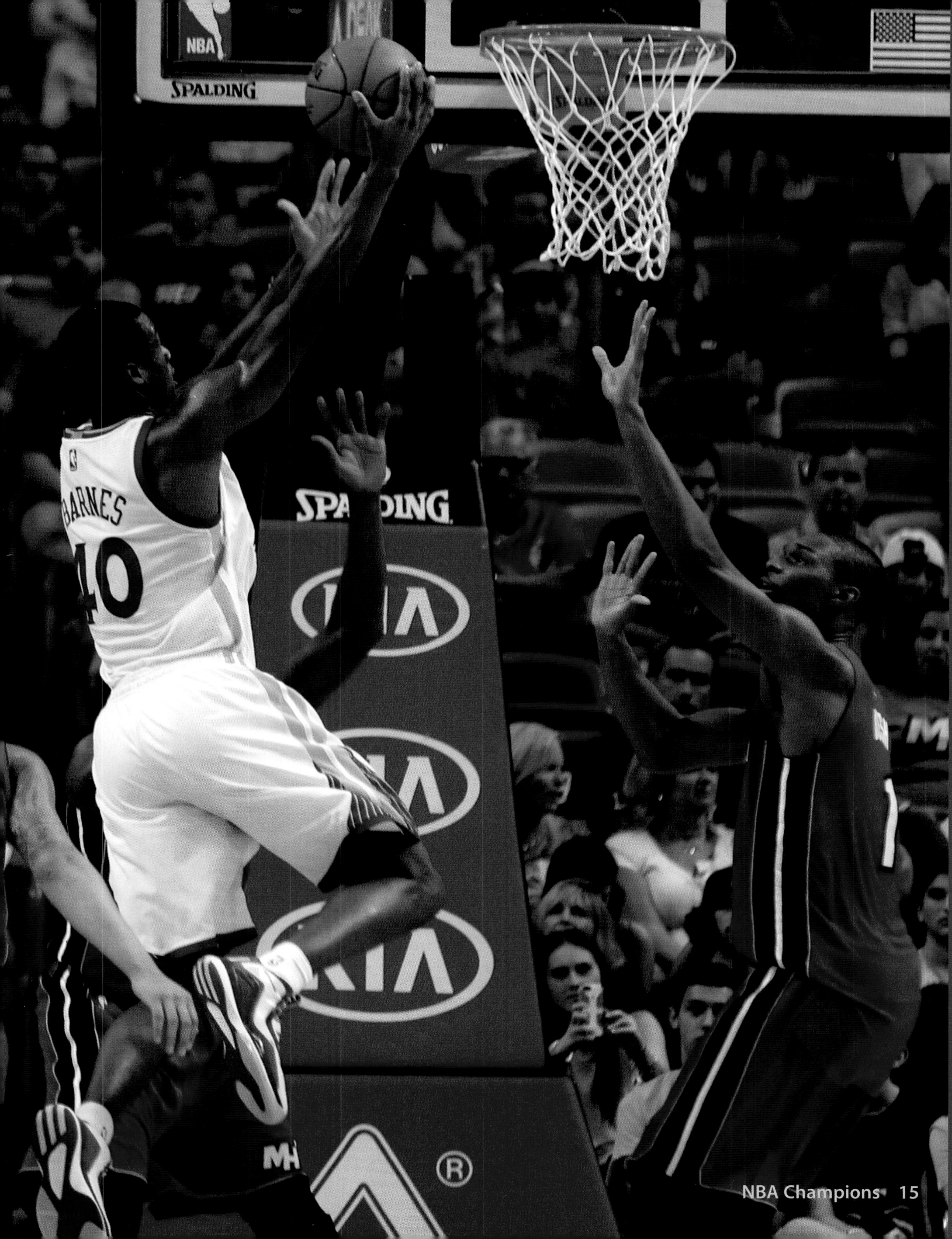
NBA
SPALDING
BARNES
40
KIA

WARRIORS 126 • KINGS 101

THOMPSON SETS SCORING RECORD ON WAY TO 52 POINT NIGHT

The sellout crowd chanted Klay Thompson's name. Both benches stood, equally stunned at what was taking place. Thompson's teammates continued to get him the ball – and he just kept shooting.

"They just kept wanting to see the show," Thompson said. "That's what they kept telling me."

Thompson set a league record for the most points in a quarter Friday night, a thrilling 37-point third period that powered the Golden State Warriors to a 126-101 victory over the Sacramento Kings.

"I was one of the luckiest NBA players ever to play with Michael Jordan, Tim Duncan, David Robinson and some of the greatest players ever," Warriors coach Steve Kerr said. "As many spectacular things as Michael did, which he did nightly, I never saw him do that."

Thompson finished with a career-high 52 points, pleasing 19,596 fans at rowdy Oracle Arena with a performance that will long be remembered in the basketball-loving Bay Area. The All-Star hopeful made all 13 shots, including a league-record nine from 3-point range in a quarter, and hit both of his free throws during a 12-minute span of pure basketball bliss.

"It was kind of a blur. I wish I could go back and enjoy it some more, but moments like that go by really fast," Thompson said.

His streaky shooting stroke helped the Warriors (35-6) erase a sloppy showing in the middle of the game for their franchise-best 18th consecutive home victory. Golden State became the 10th team to win at least 35 games halfway through a season.

Thompson surpassed the 33-point mark set by George Gervin in 1978 and matched by Carmelo Anthony in 2008 for the most points in a quarter. Michael Redd and Joe Johnson shared the previous mark for most 3s in a quarter with eight.

Thompson, who signed a four-year, near-maximum contract extension worth about $70 million this summer, couldn't remember ever dominating a game like that.

"Maybe elementary school," he joked.

A day after backcourt teammate Stephen Curry received the most All-Star votes in the NBA and Kerr learned he would lead the Western Conference in the league's showcase game, Thompson let the world know he expects to be right next to them at Madison Square Garden on Feb. 15.

Thompson stunned Sacramento – and just about everyone in the building – with a performance unlike any other in league lore. He hit one I-can't-believe-he-just-made-that basket after another – including a 28-footer – and added an alley-oop from Curry on the fast break just for good measure.

Thompson said two other shots left him just as baffled: an off-balance one in the corner, and another off a curl that got a "shooter's bounce." He even made one from about 10 feet beyond the 3-point line after a play that didn't count.

Warriors' Klay Thompson shoots during the third quarter against the Sacramento Kings on his way to a record setting night. *AP Photo | Ben Margot*

Thompson shoots over Sacramento Kings' Ray McCallum (3). *AP Photo | Ben Margot*

At that point, Warriors assistant Jarron Collins turned to Kerr and quipped, "We have to get more balance."

Thompson seemed to love every minute of it, flapping his hands to the crowd while running down the court. During one timeout, he sat on the bench with his hands over his head, staring at the scoreboard in disbelief.

"It was reminiscent of Michael (Jordan), because it was sort of otherworldly," Kerr said.

Thompson scored 19 consecutive points during one scintillating stretch, which ended with him zipping a left-handed pass to Draymond Green for a layup.

"You don't get that hot in '(NBA) 2K,'" Green said, referring to the popular video game.

Thompson finally a missed a shot – from 21 feet – at the start of the fourth quarter, in the game only because, Kerr said, players pleaded with him not to take him out. Thompson left to a standing ovation with 9:28 remaining.

"You always dream about it, being a big-time scorer and a big-time player. It's crazy it's reality," said Thompson, who finished 16-of-25 from the floor, 11-of-15 from long range and 9-of-10 on free throws.

Thompson's touch made sure the Warriors equaled the franchise's highest win total before the All-Star Game. The defending champion 1975-76 Warriors went 35-13 before the break and finished with a team-best record of 59-23.∎

Thompson, right, celebrates with Leandro Barbosa during the third quarter. Thompson set an NBA record for the highest-scoring quarter in league history, scoring 37 points in the third. *AP Photo | Ben Margot*

WARRIORS 128 • MAVERICKS 114

WARRIORS RALLY FROM 22 DOWN TO BEAT MAVERICKS

In the midst of his highest-scoring performance ever at home, Stephen Curry figured he'd call a play for someone else. Instead, teammate Draymond Green looked at him and shouted, "Get 50."

No problem.

Curry raced down the court and made his 10th 3-pointer to finish with a season-high 51 points, capping an electrifying effort that rallied the Golden State Warriors from an early 22-point deficit to defeat the Dallas Mavericks 128-114 on Wednesday night.

"Sometimes Steph plays his best when we're down big, and he just senses that he has to put the Superman cape on," Warriors coach Steve Kerr said. "And he's so good at it. He loves the freedom of being down and saying, 'All right. I'm going to let it fly and bring us back.' And that's what he did."

Curry connected on 10 of 16 shots from beyond the arc and 16 of 26 overall. The All-Star point guard and MVP candidate put on a dazzling dribbling display to match his streaky shooting stroke, scoring 26 points in the third quarter alone to help the NBA-leading Warriors (39-8) complete their biggest comeback of the season in front of a roaring sellout crowd of 19,596.

"If I had any kind of daylight off the pick-and-roll, I was going to shoot it," Curry said. "I had a good feel and a good rhythm."

Chandler Parsons scored 24 points, and Tyson Chandler had 21 points and 17 rebounds in a disappointing defeat for Dallas, which played without injured point guard Rajon Rondo again. The Mavericks led 40-18 in the first quarter before Curry carried Golden State back.

"He had one of those extra-special nights. I've never seen anybody in this league hit shots like that from that distance," Mavs coach Rick Carlisle said.

Curry finished just shy of his 54-point masterpiece at Madison Square Garden on Feb. 27, 2013. He made a career-high 11 3-pointers in that game, a 109-105 loss to the Knicks, but could savor a home victory this time.

Curry had 41 points and nine 3-pointers to give Golden State a 101-98 lead through three quarters. The Warriors stretched that margin to 112-101 early in the fourth with Curry on the bench, then called him back when the Mavericks moved within seven.

The quick-footed guard guided the Warriors in the right direction, putting the game out of reach when he chased down an errant pass by Devin Harris in the backcourt and drew a foul on Dirk Nowitzki while going for a layup. Curry made both free throws, then hit another pair the next time down to put Golden State up 124-113 with 1:35 remaining.

Curry cemented another career night with the step-back 3-pointer, setting off chants of "M-V-P! M-V-P!" throughout the building.

His hot-shooting performance only highlighted an impressive display by the Warriors, who hit 19 of 38 shots from 3-point range. The Mavericks made 10 of 30 from beyond the arc.

Klay Thompson had 18 points, and Marreese Speights and Leandro Barbosa scored 14 each off the bench as the Warriors won their third straight game. They begin a stretch of 10 of 11 on the road Friday night at East-leading Atlanta.

Warriors' Stephen Curry, right, looks for a shot as Dallas Mavericks' Al-Farouq Aminu (7) and another player defend. *AP Photo | Marcio Jose Sanchez*

Curry dribbles past Dallas Mavericks' Devin Harris. *AP Photo | Marcio Jose Sanchez*

Curry celebrates after making a 3-point basket.
AP Photo | Marcio Jose Sanchez

Dallas went ahead 24-4 in a little more than six minutes, stretched its lead to 22 and held on for a 42-25 advantage at the end of the first quarter. It was the most points the Warriors had allowed in any quarter this season.

The Warriors trimmed Dallas' lead to 62-58 at halftime and went ahead early in the third quarter, with Curry creating his own shots and bringing fans screaming out of their seats after every swish.

"It's one thing for him to hit the spot-up shots, but he hit shots in traffic, he makes tough floaters," Chandler said. "An incredible all-around game."∎

THE SPLASH BROTHERS

The Golden State Warriors' 115-100 win over the Charlotte Bobcats on Dec. 21, 2012, isn't revered in franchise history. But it is notable for one thing: It was the night Stephen Curry and Klay Thompson received their "Splash Brothers" nickname.

During the game, a writer for the Warriors website tweeted the nickname that has grown in popularity thanks to the play of the Warriors' All-Star guards.

"It's my claim to fame," Warriors.com writer Brian Witt said. "It's something no one way can take away. It's proof I lived on this earth that I created 'The Splash Brothers.'"

Curry and Thompson had combined for 25 points in that first half and made seven 3-pointers. Witt gave a quick intermission recap by tweeting out on the Warriors' handle:

> **Golden St. Warriors**
> ✔ **@warriors**
>
> **Halftime: Warriors 58 – Bobcats 49. @StephenCurry30 & Klay Thompson are a combined 7-of-11 from 3 point range #SplashBrothers**

The nickname was born and immediately caught the attention of Bay Area media and Warriors fans. Witt was playing off the old Oakland Athletics' nickname "Bash Brothers" for Mark McGwire and Jose Canseco.

"It's a pretty accurate term, I'd like to say," Curry said. "I don't think we've called each other that ever, but it's fun."

The Warriors also loved the nickname and pushed Witt to keep tweeting it out. Now, more than two years later, Curry and Thompson are often referred to as the "Splash Brothers" – and for good reason: They've combined to average just over 45 points per game this season. They are the Warriors' first All-Star duo since Tim Hardaway and Chris Mullin in 1993 and the franchise's first pair of All-Star starters since Rick Barry and Nate Thurmond in 1967.

"They look like the perfect compliment for each other," said Hall of Famer Jerry West, a Warriors consultant. "For me, it's fun. One of them [Curry] plays the game with a lot more personality. The other one [Thompson] is a lot more workmanlike.

They like each other, they know they're good for each other and they are a terrific backcourt."

Curry surpassed the Cleveland Cavaliers' LeBron James as the NBA's leading vote getter to land a Western Conference starting guard spot. It will be Curry's second straight All-Star appearance, both as a starter. He is seventh in the NBA in scoring, averaging 23.6 points, and is considered an MVP candidate.

Thompson was voted as an All-Star reserve by the conference's coaches before being named an injury replacement starter by Warriors coach Steve Kerr, who also is coaching the West All-Star team. His NBA-record 37 points and nine made 3-pointers in one quarter en route to a career-high 52 points against the Sacramento Kings on Jan. 23 helped Thompson's cause.

"Any time you have a game like that you take a step up," Curry said.

While the Splash Brothers share the same backcourt – and will compete against each other in Saturday's 3-point contest – they're different away from the court.

Curry is outgoing and is hosting an Under Armour private party with Oscar and Grammy winner Jamie Foxx during All-Star weekend. Curry also has an event endorsing the clothing company Express, which has a mammoth video billboard in New York's Times Square showing him modeling clothing and dribbling a ball.

"I'm learning a lot about the process off the court and how to manage it and when to say, 'No,'" Curry said. "I didn't know what that was like three years ago."

For Thompson, who is laid back, there is no All-Star commercial, hype or party.

When asked how his life has changed since scoring 37 in a quarter, Thompson said: "There has been a little bit of a difference on social media and some national coverage, but other than that, I still go out there and do what I do. Nothing has really changed."

Warriors teammate Draymond Green thinks Thompson would "rather float under the radar."

"I wouldn't say he's uncomfortable with [his celebrity]," Green said. "I just think he doesn't realize it. Klay will just go and walk down the street anywhere. It's like, 'Brah, you can't do that no more.'"

Warriors' Klay Thompson, left, celebrates with Stephen Curry after scoring a three pointer against Sacramento. *AP Photo | Rich Pedroncelli*

Curry and Thompson, Green said, have remained humble among their teammates.

"Who they are does a lot for the team chemistry," Green said. "When your two main guys, your two dogs, your two go-getters have attitudes like that, how can anyone else be selfish?"

The Warriors considered splitting up Curry and Thompson last offseason. The Warriors had conversations with the Minnesota Timberwolves about a blockbuster trade sending Thompson in exchange for Kevin Love. Curry told management his preference was to leave the backcourt intact.

"I gave my input on how good of a player Kevin Love is," Curry said. "There were obviously conversations. But there is something about continuity and letting Klay get to his full potential."

The Warriors opted not to make the trade and instead signed Thompson to a four-year, $70 million contact extension. The T'wolves eventually traded Love to the Cleveland Cavaliers.

"If you can maintain continuity it's always good in any organization, in any business," Warriors general manager Bob Myers said. "We knew who [Thompson] was. We didn't raise him, but he was raised within our organization. You just like to believe in your own guys and bet on your own guys."∎

WARRIORS 106 • PELICANS 99

WARRIORS HOLD OFF PELICANS IN PLAYOFF OPENER

So much for Stephen Curry's mini-shooting slump.

Curry scored 40 points on 11-of-18 shooting, and the Golden State Warriors beat the Miami Heat 114-97 on Tuesday night for their sixth consecutive victory.

"You just feel a rhythm," said Curry, who was 8-for-24 in his previous two games. "I had guys set some great screens early to kind of get me going. You start finding shots and it feels good. Even the ones I missed terribly felt good, which is pretty funny."

Klay Thompson had 24 points for the Warriors, who shot 57 percent. Curry finished 8-of-11 from 3-point range.

"You always stay confident, stay ready," Curry said. "You win games all sorts of ways with different individual performances. How we shot last game had nothing to do with this game. If we execute our offense well, you're going to get good shots."

Golden State scored 14 straight points to open a 107-95 lead with 2:50 to go. Curry and Thompson capped the run with consecutive 3-pointers.

Golden State Warriors' Stephen Curry (30) scores past New Orleans Pelicans' Alexis Ajinca (42) during the first half. *AP Photo | Marcio Jose Sanchez*

Warriors' Klay Thompson, right, shoots over New Orleans Pelicans' Norris Cole (30) and Quincy Pondexter (20) during the second half. *AP Photo | Marcio Jose Sanchez*

"The beauty of this team is we can play both ends," Warriors coach Steve Kerr said. "We have the personnel to score. We have the personnel to guard."

Chris Bosh scored 26 points for Miami, and Luol Deng had 16. James Ennis' dunk with 9:11 left was the Heat's last field goal.

"They played their best basketball in the fourth quarter," Heat coach Erik Spoelstra said. "We got caught up in some tough possessions. Their defense really stepped up and then they started to score and we just weren't able to sustain from there."

Miami led by 16 in the first half but Golden State closed the second quarter with a 23-8 surge. Draymond Green made two free throws with 9.8 seconds left to cut the Heat's lead to 62-61 at the break.

Golden state carried the momentum over to the second half. Curry hit three 3 pointers in the third period and his two free throws with 58.2 seconds remaining put Golden State head, 89-82.

"This game was a huge challenge for us, probably our biggest challenge defensively we've faced all year because they present a lot of problems," Kerr said. "Second half – everybody was

	1	2	3	4	T
New Orleans	13	28	25	33	99
Golden State	28	31	25	22	106

Top Performers

NO: A. Davis 35 Pts, 7 Reb, 1 Ast, 1 Stl, 4 Blk

GS: S. Curry 34 Pts, 4 Reb, 5 Ast, 3 Stl

PELICANS

STARTERS	MIN	FGM-A	3PM-A	FTM-A	OREB	DREB	REB	AST	STL	BLK	TO	PF	PTS
Anthony Davis, PF	40	13-23	0-1	9-10	3	4	7	1	1	4	5	4	35
Omer Asik, C	22	0-1	0-0	2-4	2	7	9	1	1	0	1	3	2
Eric Gordon, SG	35	5-14	4-7	2-2	0	2	2	3	1	0	5	4	16
Tyreke Evans, SG	12	0-2	0-0	1-2	0	1	1	0	0	0	0	0	1
Quincy Pondexter, SG	37	7-14	3-7	3-4	0	9	9	6	2	0	0	5	20

BENCH	MIN	FGM-A	3PM-A	FTM-A	OREB	DREB	REB	AST	STL	BLK	TO	PF	PTS
Ryan Anderson, PF	21	1-6	1-2	0-0	2	3	5	1	0	0	1	4	3
Dante Cunningham, PF	15	1-3	0-0	1-1	2	3	5	0	1	0	0	1	3
Alexis Ajinca, C	4	3-3	0-0	0-0	0	1	1	1	1	0	0	1	6
Norris Cole, PG	34	3-10	0-3	2-2	0	3	3	6	0	1	0	5	8
Jrue Holiday, PG	21	2-7	1-2	0-0	1	1	2	5	1	0	2	1	5
Luke Babbitt, SF					DNP COACH'S DECISION								
Jimmer Fredette, PG					DNP COACH'S DECISION								
Toney Douglas, PG					DNP COACH'S DECISION								

TOTALS		FGM-A	3PM-A	FTM-A	OREB	DREB	REB	AST	STL	BLK	TO	PF	PTS
		35-83	9-22	20-25	10	34	44	24	8	5	14	28	99
		42.2%	40.9%	80.0%									

WARRIORS

STARTERS	MIN	FGM-A	3PM-A	FTM-A	OREB	DREB	REB	AST	STL	BLK	TO	PF	PTS
Harrison Barnes, SF	31	4-8	2-3	2-2	3	5	8	1	1	0	1	2	12
Draymond Green, SF	42	5-11	1-3	4-6	1	11	12	7	3	2	3	4	15
Andrew Bogut, C	30	6-8	0-0	0-2	4	10	14	5	2	2	1	3	12
Stephen Curry, PG	40	13-25	4-13	4-7	0	4	4	5	3	0	3	4	34
Klay Thompson, SG	37	6-17	3-6	6-9	0	1	1	3	1	2	5	3	21

BENCH	MIN	FGM-A	3PM-A	FTM-A	OREB	DREB	REB	AST	STL	BLK	TO	PF	PTS
Festus Ezeli, C	3	0-0	0-0	2-2	0	0	0	0	0	0	1	0	2
Marreese Speights, C	1	0-0	0-0	0-0	0	0	0	0	0	0	0	0	0
Shaun Livingston, PG	13	1-3	0-0	0-0	0	0	0	0	0	0	1	2	2
Leandro Barbosa, SG	11	0-3	0-0	0-0	2	2	4	0	0	0	0	1	0
Andre Iguodala, SG	31	2-6	1-4	3-6	0	4	4	3	1	0	0	2	8
James Michael McAdoo, SF					DNP COACH'S DECISION								
Justin Holiday, SG					DNP COACH'S DECISION								
Brandon Rush, SG					DNP COACH'S DECISION								

TOTALS		FGM-A	3PM-A	FTM-A	OREB	DREB	REB	AST	STL	BLK	TO	PF	PTS
		37-81	11-29	21-34	10	37	47	24	11	6	15	21	106
		45.7%	37.9%	61.8%									

Flagrant Fouls: None

Technical Fouls: PLAYERS: 1 NEW ORLEANS (Pondexter 1) – TEAMS: None – COACHES: None

Officials: Jason Phillips, Tony Brothers, Sean Corbin

Attendance: 19,596

Time of Game: 2:39

more in tune. We got to their 3-point shooters. We ran them off the line. In the end, we got it rolling."

Harrison Barnes finished with 12 points and Andrew Bogut had 10 rebounds for the Warriors. Bogut started after sustaining a right orbital bone contusion on Sunday.

The Heat got off to a nice start, opening a 31-22 lead on Mario Chalmers' corner 3-pointer with 1:51 left in the first quarter.

"I don't really get what we think or what we do down the stretch against good teams, the elite teams," Bosh said. "For some reason we just forget everything – offense and defense execution." ■

WARRIORS 97 • PELICANS 87

WARRIORS RALLY TO GO UP 2-0

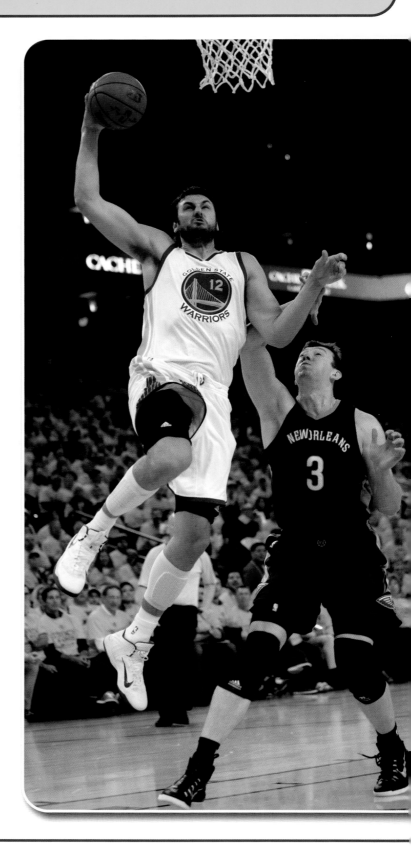

Golden State Warriors coach Steve Kerr likes to say his team teeters on "explosive and careless" basketball, pulling off an astonishing play one moment and a perplexing one the next.

Kerr saw both extremes Monday night.

And the better half was just good enough to defend home court.

Klay Thompson scored 26 points, Stephen Curry had 22 points and six assists, and the Warriors regrouped from an early deficit to beat the New Orleans Pelicans 97-87 and take a 2-0 lead in their first-round playoff series.

"We still get excited at times and do some crazy things. I kind of like the fact that we walk that line," Kerr said. "It's what makes us who we are."

The top-seeded Warriors fell behind by 13 points in the first quarter after a strong start by Anthony Davis and Eric Gordon quieted an announced sellout crowd of 19,596 wearing golden-yellow shirts. But a big burst before halftime pushed the Warriors ahead, and their defense clamped down in the closing moments to put away the pesky Pelicans.

Davis had 26 points and 10 rebounds, and Gordon scored 23 points for a Pelicans team that played with more poise and passion than it did in the series opener.

"We just have to stick with it," Gordon said.

"We're playing the best team in the league, and we're fighting tooth and nail," Pelicans coach

Warriors' Andrew Bogut (12) dunks past New Orleans Pelicans' Omer Asik (3) during the first half in Game 2. *AP Photo | Marcio Jose Sanchez*

Warriors' Festus Ezeli (31) defends on New Orleans Pelicans' Anthony Davis (23). *AP Photo | Marcio Jose Sanchez*

Monty Williams added. "Our guys are grouping up on the fly."

In the end, the Warriors were just better when it mattered most.

Golden State turned up the NBA's top-rated defense late, holding the Pelicans to 35 points in the second half. New Orleans shot just 37.8 percent for the game.

Davis still pulled the Pelicans within one in the final minutes before Draymond Green and center Andrew Bogut – Golden State's defensive stoppers – helped the Warriors shut down New Orleans again.

Thompson converted a running bank shot over

Gordon to start a three-point play, and Bogut followed with a two-handed slam to give Golden State a 97-86 lead with 1:02 left, fending off a tougher-than-expected fight from the West's eighth seed.

"We know we're going to have turnovers or lapses. But it's the defense that won us the game," Thompson said.

The Warriors have won 20 straight games and 41 of 43 at home this season. Their last loss at Oracle Arena came against Chicago in overtime on Jan. 27.

New Orleans made five of its first six shots and got big contributions from Gordon and Davis to go

Warriors' head coach Steve Kerr argues a call during the second half.
AP Photo | Marcio Jose Sanchez

	1	2	3	4	T	Top Performers
New Orleans	28	24	19	16	87	NO: A. Davis 26 Pts, 11 Reb, 3 Ast, 2 Stl, 2 Blk
Golden State	17	38	16	26	97	GS: K. Thompson 26 Pts, 3 Reb, 3 Ast, 1 Stl

PELICANS

STARTERS	MIN	FGM-A	3PM-A	FTM-A	OREB	DREB	REB	AST	STL	BLK	TO	PF	PTS
Anthony Davis, PF	45	9-22	0-0	8-8	1	10	11	3	2	2	3	3	26
Omer Asik, C	24	1-3	0-0	0-0	6	7	13	2	2	0	3	5	2
Eric Gordon, SG	39	9-18	5-10	0-0	0	0	0	2	0	0	4	2	23
Tyreke Evans, SG	41	4-13	1-3	7-12	1	9	10	7	0	1	0	1	16
Quincy Pondexter, SG	32	1-8	0-2	1-1	1	2	3	4	4	0	1	2	3

BENCH	MIN	FGM-A	3PM-A	FTM-A	OREB	DREB	REB	AST	STL	BLK	TO	PF	PTS
Ryan Anderson, PF	9	1-5	0-2	2-2	0	1	1	2	0	0	0	2	4
Dante Cunningham, PF	18	1-1	0-0	0-0	0	0	0	0	2	1	0	1	2
Alexis Ajinca, C	4	0-0	0-0	0-0	0	0	0	0	0	0	0	1	0
Norris Cole, PG	28	5-11	1-3	0-1	1	2	3	1	0	0	2	3	11
Luke Babbitt, SF					DNP COACH'S DECISION								
Jimmer Fredette, PG					DNP COACH'S DECISION								
Jrue Holiday, PG					DNP RIGHT LEG								
Toney Douglas, PG					DNP COACH'S DECISION								

TOTALS		FGM-A	3PM-A	FTM-A	OREB	DREB	REB	AST	STL	BLK	TO	PF	PTS
		31-81	7-20	18-24	10	31	41	21	10	4	13	20	87
		38.3%	35.0%	75.0%									

WARRIORS

STARTERS	MIN	FGM-A	3PM-A	FTM-A	OREB	DREB	REB	AST	STL	BLK	TO	PF	PTS
Harrison Barnes, SF	22	2-6	0-2	1-2	1	1	2	3	1	0	1	2	5
Draymond Green, SF	42	4-12	2-6	4-6	1	11	12	5	3	1	4	2	14
Andrew Bogut, C	33	2-5	0-0	1-2	4	10	14	2	1	3	2	4	5
Stephen Curry, PG	37	9-21	3-9	1-1	0	4	4	6	1	0	5	1	22
Klay Thompson, SG	33	11-17	3-8	1-1	1	2	3	3	1	0	0	3	26

BENCH	MIN	FGM-A	3PM-A	FTM-A	OREB	DREB	REB	AST	STL	BLK	TO	PF	PTS
Festus Ezeli, C	3	0-1	0-0	0-0	2	0	2	0	0	0	0	1	0
Marreese Speights, C	13	2-7	0-0	1-2	2	2	4	1	1	2	0	1	5
Shaun Livingston, PG	13	1-2	0-0	1-2	0	1	1	4	0	0	0	1	3
Leandro Barbosa, SG	15	5-8	0-1	2-3	1	0	1	1	0	0	1	1	12
Andre Iguodala, SG	30	2-7	1-4	0-0	2	4	6	2	0	0	0	2	5
James Michael McAdoo, SF					DNP COACH'S DECISION								
Justin Holiday, SG					DNP COACH'S DECISION								
Brandon Rush, SG					DNP COACH'S DECISION								

TOTALS		FGM-A	3PM-A	FTM-A	OREB	DREB	REB	AST	STL	BLK	TO	PF	PTS
		38-86	9-30	12-19	14	35	49	27	8	6	13	18	97
		44.2%	30.0%	63.2%									

Flagrant Fouls: None
Technical Fouls: PLAYERS: None – TEAMS: None – COACHES: None
Officials: Sean Wright, Joe Crawford, Ron Garretson
Attendance: 19,596
Time of Game: 2:19

ahead 28-17 after the first quarter. Reserve guard Leandro Barbosa (12 points) and the backups brought the Warriors back in the second quarter.

Of course, the Pelicans struggled to corral Curry and Thompson in the key moments.

They helped the Warriors outscore New Orleans 38-24 in the second quarter, with Curry capping the run with a deep 3-pointer to give Golden State a 55-52 halftime lead. The Warriors went up by nine early in the third quarter, and the teams were tied 71-all entering the fourth. ∎

WARRIORS 123 • PELICANS 119

CURRY LEADS 4TH QUARTER COMEBACK – WARRIORS UP 3-0

Stephen Curry wasn't about to turn down the music or put any kind of damper on a giddy locker room celebration that seemed more reminiscent of a series-clinching triumph.

The Golden State Warriors still need one more victory to close out their first-round playoff series with New Orleans, yet couldn't help but exchange congratulatory embraces after the stunning, character-defining rally they pulled off in Game 3.

Curry scored 40 points, including a 3-pointer in the final seconds of regulation to complete a 20-point, fourth-quarter comeback, and the Warriors beat the Pelicans 123-119 in overtime Thursday night to take a 3-0 series lead.

"You know how big of a deal it is to come back from a deficit like that in the playoffs on the road, in a game we knew was very important for us to really take control of this series," Curry said. "So I think we should celebrate the accomplishment."

Curry hit seven 3s, including one to start overtime that gave the Warriors the lead for good.

Klay Thompson had 28 points for the Warriors, who trailed 89-69 after three quarters, then outscored New Orleans 39-19 over the next 12 minutes.

"We haven't been in that position a lot this year, but mental toughness and resilience is

Warriors guard Stephen Curry celebrates the Warriors' 123-119 overtime victory over the New Orleans Pelicans in Game 3. *AP Photo | Gerald Herbert*

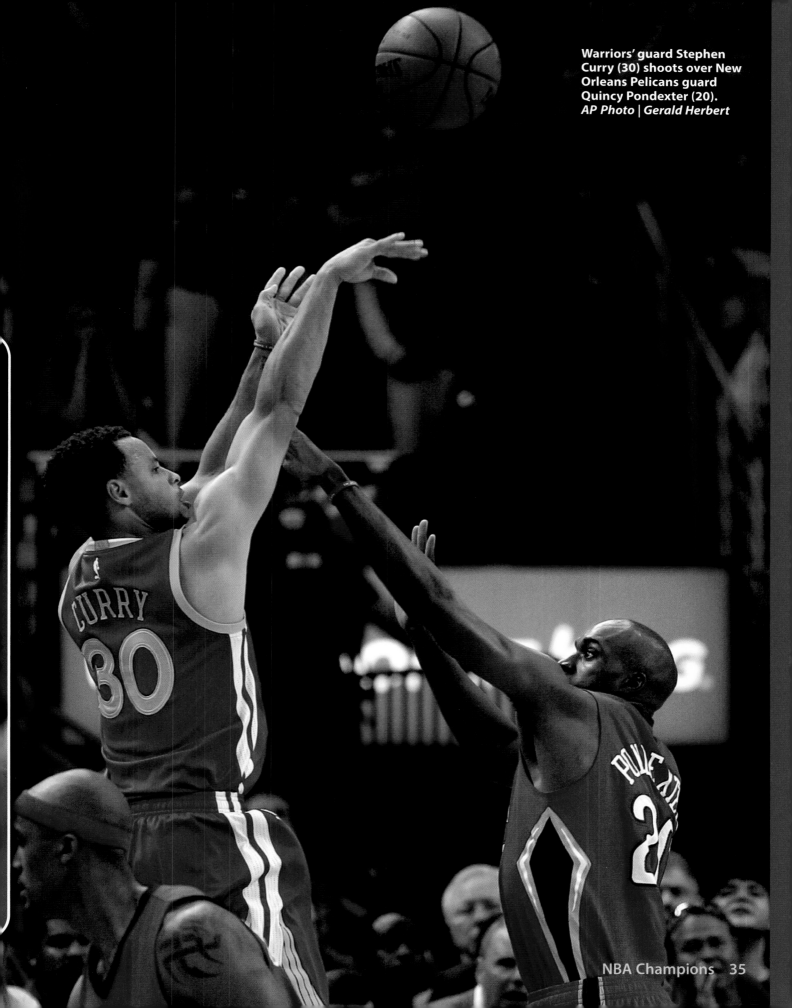

Warriors' guard Stephen Curry (30) shoots over New Orleans Pelicans guard Quincy Pondexter (20).
AP Photo | Gerald Herbert

▲Warriors forward Harrison Barnes (40) dunks the ball around New Orleans Pelicans guard Quincy Pondexter (20). *AP Photo | Icon Sportswire*

▶New Orleans Pelicans guard Norris Cole (30) shoots over Golden State Warriors forward Draymond Green (23) during the game. *AP Photo | Cal Sports Media*

probably (among) our best traits," Thompson said. "It was an amazing way to finish the game."

Golden State coach Steve Kerr called the comeback miraculous, and at least one statistic provided by the Warriors backed him up.

Since the NBA instituted the shot clock, Golden State had been down 20 to start a fourth quarter 358 previous times – and won none of those games.

Now the Warriors can end the series in Game 4 on Saturday night.

Anthony Davis had 29 points and 15 rebounds for the Pelicans, but his missed free throw with 9.6 seconds left – as the crowd chanted "M-V-P!" – allowed Curry's late 3 to tie it.

The Pelicans expected Curry to shoot, and his first attempt in the final seconds bounced out. But Marreese Speights corralled the offensive rebound and handed it to Curry in the corner. The Warriors' sharpshooter wasn't going to miss twice, not even

	1	2	3	4	OT	T	Top Performers
Golden State	25	27	17	39	15	123	GS: S. Curry 40 Pts, 5 Reb, 9 Ast
New Orleans	26	37	26	19	11	119	NO: A. Davis 29 Pts, 15 Reb, 3 Ast, 2 Stl, 3 Blk

WARRIORS

STARTERS	MIN	FGM-A	3PM-A	FTM-A	OREB	DREB	REB	AST	STL	BLK	TO	PF	PTS
Harrison Barnes, SF	37	4-9	1-2	2-2	4	3	7	2	1	2	0	1	11
Draymond Green, SF	40	5-11	0-2	2-3	7	10	17	5	3	1	1	6	12
Andrew Bogut, C	26	3-5	0-0	0-0	2	3	5	1	0	0	2	2	6
Stephen Curry, PG	44	10-29	7-18	13-14	1	4	5	9	0	0	3	3	40
Klay Thompson, SG	46	9-21	6-12	4-5	1	5	6	2	0	2	2	3	28

BENCH	MIN	FGM-A	3PM-A	FTM-A	OREB	DREB	REB	AST	STL	BLK	TO	PF	PTS
Festus Ezeli, C	4	1-1	0-0	0-0	1	1	2	0	0	0	0	0	2
Marreese Speights, C	11	1-7	0-0	0-0	3	1	4	1	0	1	1	4	2
Shaun Livingston, PG	20	5-7	0-0	2-3	3	1	4	0	0	0	0	2	12
Leandro Barbosa, SG	11	2-6	0-2	2-2	0	0	0	0	0	0	1	0	6
Andre Iguodala, SG	26	2-8	0-5	0-1	0	1	1	4	0	0	0	1	4
David Lee, PF					DNP COACH'S DECISION								
Justin Holiday, SG					DNP COACH'S DECISION								
Brandon Rush, SG					DNP COACH'S DECISION								

TOTALS		FGM-A	3PM-A	FTM-A	OREB	DREB	REB	AST	STL	BLK	TO	PF	PTS
		42-104	14-41	25-30	22	29	51	24	4	6	10	22	123
		40.4%	34.1%	83.3%									

PELICANS

STARTERS	MIN	FGM-A	3PM-A	FTM-A	OREB	DREB	REB	AST	STL	BLK	TO	PF	PTS
Anthony Davis, PF	46	11-22	0-0	7-9	3	12	15	3	2	3	4	4	29
Omer Asik, C	20	0-2	0-0	1-2	3	3	6	1	1	0	1	1	1
Eric Gordon, SG	35	2-10	1-6	1-2	1	3	4	5	1	2	0	3	6
Tyreke Evans, SG	40	8-18	1-6	2-3	0	4	4	8	3	0	4	5	19
Quincy Pondexter, SG	35	2-4	0-1	2-2	2	4	6	2	0	0	0	4	6

BENCH	MIN	FGM-A	3PM-A	FTM-A	OREB	DREB	REB	AST	STL	BLK	TO	PF	PTS
Ryan Anderson, PF	30	10-14	2-3	4-4	3	2	5	2	0	0	2	3	26
Dante Cunningham, PF	16	3-3	0-0	0-0	0	5	5	0	0	2	0	2	6
Norris Cole, PG	26	5-11	1-3	0-1	1	2	3	1	0	0	2	3	11
Jrue Holiday, PG	17	3-7	0-1	4-4	1	0	1	4	0	1	1	2	10
Luke Babbitt, SF					DNP COACH'S DECISION								
Alexis Ajinca, C					DNP COACH'S DECISION								
Jimmer Fredette, PG					DNP COACH'S DECISION								
Toney Douglas, PG					DNP COACH'S DECISION								

TOTALS		FGM-A	3PM-A	FTM-A	OREB	DREB	REB	AST	STL	BLK	TO	PF	PTS
		46-90	6-21	21-26	13	34	47	25	7	8	14	28	119
		51.1%	28.6%	80.8%									

Flagrant Fouls: None
Technical Fouls: PLAYERS: 1 NEW ORLEANS (Pondexter 1) – TEAMS: None – COACHES: None
Officials: Derrick Stafford, Kane Fitzgerald, Scott Foster
Attendance: 18,444
Time of Game: 2:57

with defenders, including Davis, closing fast and running into him on his follow-through.

Kerr called the shot "as good as it gets."

"To make that shot shows everything that Steph is about," Kerr said, adding that officials could have called a foul, too. "His confidence level is just off the charts. He's fearless. He wants every big shot."

Draymond Green had 12 points and 17 rebounds for Golden State, which finished with 22 offensive rebounds and 30 second-chance points.■

WARRIORS 109 ● PELICANS 98

SWEEP COMPLETE

Stephen Curry wasn't about to say that shooting over Anthony Davis was easy.

The Warriors' prolific scorer was just crafty enough to make it look that way sometimes.

Equally devastating from long range and on drives to the hoop, Curry scored 39 points, and the Golden State Warriors took a 109-98 victory over the New Orleans Pelicans on Saturday night, completing a sweep of their first-round playoff series.

"I knew he was crafty, I mean, a great shooter," Davis said of Curry, who averaged 33.8 points in the series. "There's nothing you can do. You try to pressure him and run him off the [3-point] line and he'll hit incredible shots in the lane. You back off so he won't drive, he's going to hit a 3. So you've got to pick your poison, and he's a tough player to guard. That's why he's [a candidate] for MVP."

Klay Thompson added 25 points for the Warriors, the NBA's top overall seed, who will wait to host Game 1 of their second-round series against the winner of the Portland-Memphis matchup.

"I'm proud of the way we played, the way we competed," Curry said. "Four in a row is a good feeling. We're going to rest up."

Draymond Green added 22 points and 10 rebounds for Golden State, which raced to a 67-54 halftime lead and widened the gap to as many as 24 points in the second half before the desperate Pelicans briefly cut their deficit to single digits in the final minutes.

Curry had eight rebounds and nine assists in Game 4.

Warriors' guard Klay Thompson (11) shoots against New Orleans Pelicans' guard Eric Gordon (10) during the second half. *AP Photo | Gerald Herbert*

Warriors' guard Stephen Curry (30) shoot a lay up around New Orleans Pelicans forward Anthony Davis (23).
AP Photo | Cal Sport Media

"What we've been through playing against Steph sometimes, it's not fair," Pelicans coach Monty Williams said. "Steph is like, he's on a different level -- some of the shots he makes, his command of the ball, his ability to finish. The moment doesn't bother him.

"He is in the elite of the elite right now, and he's after something and you can tell by the way he's playing."

Davis had 36 points and 11 rebounds to close out what has been a remarkable third season for the Pelicans' 22-year-old franchise player. He just didn't have quite enough help on either end of the court.

The 6-foot-10 Davis is one of few big men quick and agile enough to guard the NBA's top perimeter players, and he usually has a height advantage about as significant as the 7 inches he had on Curry.

"We had a couple sets that we tried to get him away from the basket so that we could attack the paint," Curry said. "Tonight, a couple times, I just tried to go one-on-one and get some space. He's very long, obviously, and can contest a lot of

Warriors' forward Draymond Green (23) takes a shoot over an outstretched New Orleans Pelicans' forward Anthony Davis (23). *AP Photo | Gerald Herbert*

	1	2	3	4	T	Top Performers
Golden State	31	36	21	21	109	GS: S. Curry 39 Pts, 8 Reb, 9 Ast, 1 Stl
New Orleans	24	30	13	31	98	NO: A. Davis 36 Pts, 11 Reb, 1 Ast, 3 Blk

WARRIORS

STARTERS	MIN	FGM-A	3PM-A	FTM-A	OREB	DREB	REB	AST	STL	BLK	TO	PF	PTS
Harrison Barnes, SF	35	3-7	0-0	0-2	2	6	8	3	1	1	0	0	6
Draymond Green, SF	42	9-14	3-6	1-2	3	7	10	8	1	1	2	4	22
Andrew Bogut, C	22	1-1	0-0	0-0	0	3	3	1	0	3	1	5	2
Stephen Curry, PG	38	11-20	6-8	11-12	3	5	8	9	1	0	5	4	39
Klay Thompson, SG	36	10-19	4-7	1-1	0	3	3	0	1	1	0	0	25
BENCH	MIN	FGM-A	3PM-A	FTM-A	OREB	DREB	REB	AST	STL	BLK	TO	PF	PTS
Festus Ezeli, C	9	0-2	0-0	1-4	1	2	3	0	0	0	1	1	1
Marreese Speights, C	4	0-1	0-0	0-0	0	1	1	1	0	0	0	0	0
Shaun Livingston, PG	17	0-2	0-0	0-0	0	1	1	3	1	1	0	1	0
Leandro Barbosa, SG	11	3-5	0-0	0-0	0	0	0	1	0	0	1	1	6
Andre Iguodala, SG	24	3-8	0-3	2-2	1	1	2	2	1	0	0	2	8
David Lee, PF					DNP COACH'S DECISION								
Justin Holiday, SG					DNP COACH'S DECISION								
Brandon Rush, SG					DNP COACH'S DECISION								
TOTALS		FGM-A	3PM-A	FTM-A	OREB	DREB	REB	AST	STL	BLK	TO	PF	PTS
		40-79	13-24	16-23	10	29	39	28	6	7	10	18	109
		50.6%	54.2%	69.6%									

PELICANS

STARTERS	MIN	FGM-A	3PM-A	FTM-A	OREB	DREB	REB	AST	STL	BLK	TO	PF	PTS
Anthony Davis, PF	40	14-20	0-1	8-9	2	9	11	1	0	3	1	1	36
Omer Asik, C	14	1-4	0-0	1-1	1	0	1	2	1	0	0	1	3
Eric Gordon, SG	35	12-21	3-9	2-2	1	2	3	5	0	0	1	2	29
Tyreke Evans, SG	33	2-10	0-2	0-0	2	3	5	5	2	0	2	4	4
Quincy Pondexter, SG	21	0-2	0-0	0-0	0	2	2	0	1	0	0	2	0
BENCH	MIN	FGM-A	3PM-A	FTM-A	OREB	DREB	REB	AST	STL	BLK	TO	PF	PTS
Ryan Anderson, PF	35	4-11	2-5	0-0	2	4	6	4	0	2	1	3	10
Dante Cunningham, PF	26	4-4	0-0	2-2	2	6	8	2	0	1	0	3	10
Alexis Ajinca, C	2	1-1	0-0	0-0	0	0	0	0	0	0	0	0	2
Norris Cole, PG	18	0-5	0-4	0-0	0	0	0	0	0	0	4	3	0
Jrue Holiday, PG	17	2-5	0-1	0-0	0	0	0	4	1	0	2	0	4
Luke Babbitt, SF					DNP COACH'S DECISION								
Jimmer Fredette, PG					DNP COACH'S DECISION								
Toney Douglas, PG					DNP COACH'S DECISION								
TOTALS		FGM-A	3PM-A	FTM-A	OREB	DREB	REB	AST	STL	BLK	TO	PF	PTS
		40-83	5-22	13-14	10	26	36	23	5	6	11	19	98
		51.1%	28.6%	80.8%									

Flagrant Fouls: None
Technical Fouls: PLAYERS: None – TEAMS: None – COACHES: None
Officials: Derrick Collins, Dan Crawford, Marc Davis
Attendance: 18,443
Time of Game: 2:19

shots, but I found a little bit of daylight."

Golden State shot 50.6 percent, including 13-of-24 from 3-point range. Curry was 6-of-8 from deep, while Thompson was 4-of-7 and Green 3-of-6.

"The first three games all came down to the wire, and then I thought tonight was our best effort of the series," Warriors coach Steve Kerr said. "I'm very pleased with the effort, and I'm very pleased I don't have to see Anthony Davis until November at the earliest."■

STEPHEN CURRY: MVP

Golden State Warriors point guard Stephen Curry has been named the Most Valuable Player for the 2014-15 NBA season, the NBA announced on Monday. The announcement caps off what was an incredible regular season for Curry, who led the Warriors to the league's best record and now hopes to reach similar heights this postseason.

Curry received 100 first place votes. James Harden of the Houston Rockets, who finished second in the voting, received 25. LeBron James finished third in the voting and Russell Westbrook finished in fourth.

Curry, 27, has emerged as the NBA's most gifted shooter the past few years . The league leader in three-pointers attempted and made over each of the past three seasons, Curry is willing to fire it up – and make it – from pretty much anywhere on the court.

Improving his ballhandling and understanding of the game over the past couple seasons, Curry has become almost impossible to guard. He can use a dribble-drive to blow right by a defender if he gets too close, and will make you pay with the jumper if you give him too much room.

The result was a dazzling performance from Curry during the 2014-15 season as everything came together. The star guard averaged nearly 24 points, eight assists and two steals over 80 games, and helped lead Golden State to a franchise-record 67 wins. This year's Warriors are one of the best teams in recent memory, and Curry has been the driving force behind that ongoing domination.

Steph Curry of the Golden State Warriors receives the 2014-15 NBA Most Valuable Player Award on May 04, 2015 in Oakland, California. *AP Photo | Cal Sport Media*

Warriors guard Stephen Curry acknowledges the crowd during a ceremony for winning the NBA's Most Valuable Player award before Game 2 in a second-round NBA playoff. *AP Photo | Jeff Chiu*

Curry's shooting numbers might be most impressive, though. The 6'3 shooting guard took 8.1 three-pointers per game and hit 44 percent of them. Nearly half of his 16.8 shots per game came from behind the arc, and yet he still managed to shoot nearly 50 percent on the season.

Nobody in the league can match those numbers, and his 63.8 true shooting percentage – which seeks to boil various shooting numbers down to a single figure – was sixth among players to play 50 or more games. The guys ahead of him were a pair of big men who do little else but dunk (Tyson Chandler, DeAndre Jordan), a pair of guys who didn't play much (Brandan Wright, Luke Babbitt) and arguably the best non-Curry shooter of the generation (Kyle Korver). None of those guys were being asked to run the offense and take nearly 20 shots a game, either.

So it's pretty easy to see what made Curry's season so special, and now the voters have rewarded him with his first NBA MVP. He had to beat out several other impressive candidates, including LeBron James, James Harden, Anthony Davis and Russell Westbrook, but it's hard to disagree with the choice.

Curry is also the first member of the Warriors to win the award since the franchise moved to San Francisco. Wilt Chamberlain won MVP as a member of the Philadelphia Warriors in 1960, two years before their move.■

WARRIORS 101 • GRIZZLIES 86

WARRIORS ROLL GRIZZLIES IN SERIES OPENER

Golden State Warriors coach Steve Kerr joked before Game 1 of the Western Conference semifinals that reporters should have two stories ready: One if his team looked well-rested and won, another if it looked rusty and lost.

"It was right in the middle, so you've got to write a third story," he teased afterward.

Neither the Warriors nor Grizzlies really felt good about the way they played. The difference is the Warriors did what they usually do at home: take care of business – and comfortably, too.

Stephen Curry had 22 points and seven assists, and the Warriors wore down undermanned Memphis in a 101-86 victory in Sunday's series opener.

"I think now we've got the cobwebs out of our offensive game. We should be able to build some momentum," Curry said.

Klay Thompson added 18 points and Draymond Green scored 16 to help the top-seeded Warriors roll to their 21st straight win at raucous Oracle Arena. They led by nine at the half, 20 late in the third quarter and never let the Grizzlies come close in the fourth despite Green and center Andrew Bogut getting in foul trouble.

Warriors' guard Klay Thompson (11) dribbles against Memphis Grizzlies' forward Tony Allen, center, and forward Zach Randolph (50) during the first half. *AP Photo | Jeff Chiu*

Warriors' guard Stephen Curry (30) shoots a three point basket, which he made, in front of Memphis Grizzlies forward Jeff Green (32). *AP Photo | Marcio Jose Sanchez*

Warriors' forward Draymond Green (23) shoots a layup over Memphis Grizzlies' center Marc Gasol (33).
AP Photo | USA Today - Kyle Terada

Marc Gasol had 21 points and nine rebounds, and Zach Randolph finished with 20 points and nine rebounds for a Memphis team missing point guard Mike Conley.

The Grizzlies could use all the help they can get right now. Curry, the MVP favorite, got off to a slow start before joining the sweet-shooting performance Golden State put on in front of its home crowd.

The Warriors shot 50.6 percent, including 46.4 percent from 3-point range (13-of-28), to keep fans that formed a sea of golden yellow shirts roaring all afternoon. Memphis shot 45.2 percent but was

just 3-of-12 (25 percent) from beyond the arc. Both teams had 16 turnovers.

"I didn't think the game was physical at all," Gasol said. "We didn't bring it to that point yet. I hope, the next game, we have to bring it to our advantage."

The Warriors, coming off a first-round sweep of New Orleans that earned them an eight-day layoff, picked up right where they left off.

Curry pushed the pace from start to finish, and the Grizzlies never could slow Golden State down. The Warriors went ahead by 16 in the second quarter, and Curry kept the pressure after

	1	2	3	4	T
Memphis	25	27	14	20	86
Golden State	32	29	22	18	101

Top Performers

Mem: Z. Randolph 20 Pts, 9 Reb, 5 Ast

GS: S. Curry 22 Pts, 2 Reb, 7 Ast, 4 Stl

GRIZZLIES

STARTERS	MIN	FGM-A	3PM-A	FTM-A	OREB	DREB	REB	AST	STL	BLK	TO	PF	PTS
Zach Randolph, PF	36	9-15	0-0	2-2	3	6	9	5	0	0	1	4	20
Tony Allen, SF	38	6-11	0-0	3-4	2	2	4	3	3	0	0	3	15
Marc Gasol, C	38	5-10	0-1	11-12	1	8	9	3	3	0	3	3	21
Courtney Lee, SG	36	4-9	1-3	0-0	0	2	2	2	0	0	3	2	9
Nick Calathes, SG	21	0-4	0-1	0-2	0	1	1	2	3	0	3	2	0

BENCH	MIN	FGM-A	3PM-A	FTM-A	OREB	DREB	REB	AST	STL	BLK	TO	PF	PTS
JaMychal Green, PF	1	0-0	0-0	0-0	0	1	1	0	0	0	0	0	0
Jeff Green, SF	27	4-9	0-1	1-2	0	2	2	4	1	0	3	0	9
Kosta Koufos, C	6	0-0	0-0	0-0	0	4	4	1	0	0	0	1	0
Russ Smith, PG	1	0-0	0-0	0-0	0	0	0	1	0	0	0	0	0
Beno Udrih, PG	19	3-7	1-3	0-0	0	1	1	1	1	0	1	1	7
Jordan Adams, SG	1	1-1	1-1	0-0	0	0	0	0	0	0	0	0	3
Vince Carter, SG	18	1-7	0-2	0-0	1	3	4	2	2	0	1	0	2
Jon Leuer, PF					DNP COACH'S DECISION								

TOTALS		FGM-A	3PM-A	FTM-A	OREB	DREB	REB	AST	STL	BLK	TO	PF	PTS
		33-73	3-12	17-22	7	30	37	24	13	0	15	16	86
		45.2%	25.0%	77.3%									

WARRIORS

STARTERS	MIN	FGM-A	3PM-A	FTM-A	OREB	DREB	REB	AST	STL	BLK	TO	PF	PTS
Harrison Barnes, SF	25	4-4	1-1	2-2	2	1	3	3	0	1	0	2	11
Draymond Green, SF	27	5-11	4-8	2-2	0	5	5	3	2	0	3	4	16
Andrew Bogut, C	24	2-3	0-1	0-0	0	6	6	1	2	0	0	6	4
Stephen Curry, PG	38	8-18	4-8	2-2	1	1	2	7	4	0	4	1	22
Klay Thompson, SG	38	8-16	2-5	0-0	0	3	3	6	1	0	4	1	18

BENCH	MIN	FGM-A	3PM-A	FTM-A	OREB	DREB	REB	AST	STL	BLK	TO	PF	PTS
David Lee, PF	4	0-3	0-0	0-0	2	0	2	0	0	0	0	0	0
James Michael McAdoo, SF	1	0-1	0-0	0-0	0	1	1	0	0	0	0	0	0
Festus Ezeli, C	11	2-2	0-0	0-0	1	2	3	0	0	1	0	0	4
Marreese Speights, C	13	4-6	0-0	2-5	0	5	5	0	1	0	1	4	10
Shaun Livingston, PG	16	1-1	0-0	0-0	1	3	4	2	0	0	1	1	2
Justin Holiday, SG	1	0-0	0-0	0-0	0	0	0	0	0	0	0	0	0
Leandro Barbosa, SG	14	2-3	1-1	1-2	0	0	0	2	0	0	1	1	6
Andre Iguodala, SG	30	3-9	1-4	1-2	0	5	5	2	3	0	1	0	8

TOTALS		FGM-A	3PM-A	FTM-A	OREB	DREB	REB	AST	STL	BLK	TO	PF	PTS
		39-77	13-28	10-15	7	32	39	26	13	2	15	20	101
		50.6%	46.4%	66.7%									

Flagrant Fouls: None

Technical Fouls: PLAYERS: None – TEAMS: None – COACHES: None

Officials: Sean Wright, Joe Crawford, Tom Washington

Attendance: 19,596

Time of Game: 2:15

Memphis moved within seven.

At one point in the third quarter, he crossed over Randolph, stepped back for a 3 and ran down court with his arms extended after the ball swished through to give Golden State an 80-60 lead.

The Grizzlies missed a chance to surge back when Bogut and Green got in foul trouble late, sending the defensive duo to the bench. Memphis never could put together a big push against Curry and company, with Gasol and Randolph coming out in the last few minutes to rest up for Game 2.∎

WARRIORS 90 • GRIZZLIES 97

CONLEY SPARKS GRIZZLIES TO EVEN SERIES 1-1

The masked man came to the rescue for the Memphis Grizzlies.

Mike Conley returned just eight days after having facial surgery to score 22 points, and the Grizzlies used a smothering defensive effort to beat the Golden State Warriors 97-90 on Tuesday night, evening the Western Conference semifinals 1-1.

Wearing the clear mask to protect his swollen face and red left eye, Conley stole the spotlight from newly minted MVP Stephen Curry. He made his first four shots to get the Grizzlies going, and Memphis did the rest on defense.

Zach Randolph had 20 points and seven rebounds, and Marc Gasol and Courtney Lee scored 15 points each to help the Grizzlies end Golden State's 21-game home-winning streak. The Warriors dropped to 42-3 this season at rowdy Oracle Arena, losing for the first time at home in more than three months.

"Tremendous heart," Grizzlies coach Dave Joerger said of his point guard's effort. "He gave us an extra element."

Memphis rallied behind its banged-up floor leader, scoring the final nine points of the first half to take a 50-39 lead. It was only the second time this season the Warriors were held under 40 points in the first half.

Warriors' center Andrew Bogut (12) blocks a shot attempt by Memphis Grizzlies' guard Courtney Lee (5) as forward David Lee (10) follows. *AP Photo | Jeff Chiu*

Memphis Grizzlies' guard Mike Conley (11) drives on Warriors' guard Leandro Barbosa (19) during the first half.
AP Photo | Ben Margot

When the Warriors started to rally in the fourth quarter, Conley came through again. He made a 3-pointer to give the Grizzlies a 90-80 lead with 2:11 left, silencing the sea of golden yellow shirts for good.

Conley, who had three assists in 27 minutes,

cramped up and went to the bench briefly in the final minutes.

By that point, his job was done.

Curry collected 19 points, six assists and five rebounds but had little help from backcourt teammate Klay Thompson, who was smothered by

Warriors' guard Stephen Curry, center, shoots against Memphis Grizzlies' forward Tony Allen (9), forward Zach Randolph (50) and center Marc Gasol (33) during the second half. *AP Photo | Jeff Chiu*

	1	2	3	4	T
Memphis	28	22	23	27	97
Golden State	22	17	24	27	90

Top Performers
Mem: Z. Randolph 20 Pts, 7 Reb, 4 Ast, 1 Stl
GS: S. Curry 19 Pts, 5 Reb, 6 Ast

GRIZZLIES

STARTERS	MIN	FGM-A	3PM-A	FTM-A	OREB	DREB	REB	AST	STL	BLK	TO	PF	PTS
Zach Randolph, PF	36	7-16	0-0	6-6	2	5	7	4	1	0	2	4	20
Tony Allen, SF	37	4-7	0-1	1-1	1	3	4	2	4	1	3	3	9
Marc Gasol, C	31	5-10	0-0	5-6	0	6	6	3	2	0	3	5	15
Mike Conley, PG	27	8-12	3-6	3-4	0	0	0	3	0	0	1	1	22
Courtney Lee, SG	33	5-13	2-4	3-3	1	1	2	1	2	0	0	3	15

BENCH	MIN	FGM-A	3PM-A	FTM-A	OREB	DREB	REB	AST	STL	BLK	TO	PF	PTS
Jeff Green, SF	26	4-10	0-2	0-0	3	3	6	1	0	0	2	0	8
Kosta Koufos, C	11	1-3	0-0	0-0	0	2	2	0	1	1	0	1	2
Beno Udrih, PG	21	2-8	0-1	0-0	0	5	5	2	2	0	1	3	4
Vince Carter, SG	18	1-4	0-1	0-0	1	6	7	3	1	0	1	1	2
Nick Calathes, SG	0	0-0	0-0	0-0	0	0	0	0	0	0	0	0	0
Jon Leuer, PF		DNP COACH'S DECISION											
JaMychal Green, PF		DNP COACH'S DECISION											
Jordan Adams, SG		DNP COACH'S DECISION											

TOTALS		FGM-A	3PM-A	FTM-A	OREB	DREB	REB	AST	STL	BLK	TO	PF	PTS
		37-83	5-15	18-20	8	31	39	19	13	2	13	21	97
		44.6%	33.3%	90.0%									

WARRIORS

STARTERS	MIN	FGM-A	3PM-A	FTM-A	OREB	DREB	REB	AST	STL	BLK	TO	PF	PTS
Harrison Barnes, SF	35	4-8	0-2	3-3	0	4	4	0	1	1	2	2	11
Draymond Green, SF	38	3-11	0-3	8-10	4	8	12	1	2	0	3	5	14
Andrew Bogut, C	24	4-5	0-0	0-0	4	8	12	2	1	1	2	2	8
Stephen Curry, PG	41	7-19	2-11	3-4	0	5	5	6	0	0	3	0	19
Klay Thompson, SG	34	6-15	1-6	0-0	0	4	4	2	1	1	5	3	13

BENCH	MIN	FGM-A	3PM-A	FTM-A	OREB	DREB	REB	AST	STL	BLK	TO	PF	PTS
David Lee, PF	5	0-2	0-0	1-2	0	2	2	0	0	0	0	0	1
Festus Ezeli, C	5	0-0	0-0	1-2	0	0	0	0	0	0	0	0	1
Marreese Speights, C	5	0-1	0-0	2-2	0	1	1	0	0	0	1	1	2
Shaun Livingston, PG	13	0-1	0-0	0-0	0	0	0	1	1	0	2	1	0
Leandro Barbosa, SG	14	5-9	1-2	3-3	1	1	2	1	0	0	1	2	14
Andre Iguodala, SG	27	2-3	2-2	1-2	0	3	3	3	0	0	1	2	7
James Michael McAdoo, SF		DNP COACH'S DECISION											
Justin Holiday, SG		DNP COACH'S DECISION											

TOTALS		FGM-A	3PM-A	FTM-A	OREB	DREB	REB	AST	STL	BLK	TO	PF	PTS
		31-74	6-26	22-28	9	36	45	16	6	3	20	18	90
		41.9%	23.1%	78.6%									

Flagrant Fouls: None
Technical Fouls: PLAYERS: 1 GOLDEN STATE (Green 1) – TEAMS: None – COACHES: None
Officials: Jason Phillips, Bill Kennedy, Scott Foster
Attendance: 19,596
Time of Game: 2:32

Allen's aggressive play. The Warriors had 20 turnovers and shot just 41.9 percent, including 23.1 percent from 3-point range. The Grizzlies had 13 steals.

"I thought we lost our poise tonight. We were in such a rush," Warriors coach Steve Kerr said.

Golden State had not lost at home since a 113-111 overtime defeat to Chicago on Jan. 27. The only other home loss came to San Antonio on Nov. 11.

"We're not going to overreact to one bad shooting night," Curry said."■

WARRIORS 89 • GRIZZLIES 99

GRIZZLIES POWER WAY TO SERIES LEAD

Steve Kerr says his Golden State Warriors are going through a learning process as a very young team.

The Memphis Grizzlies are using their hefty postseason experience to make the lesson as painful as possible.

Zach Randolph scored 22 points and Marc Gasol added 21 points and 15 rebounds as the Grizzlies beat the Warriors 99-89 on Saturday night to take a 2-1 lead in their Western Conference semifinal.

"This was a huge win for our franchise, a huge win for our team," Memphis coach Dave Joerger said. "The crowd was fantastic."

Mike Conley and Courtney Lee both finished with 11 points for Memphis, which has yet to lose this postseason with Conley in the lineup.

MVP Stephen Curry finished with 23 points for Golden State but was 8-of-21 from the field, including 2-of-10 outside the arc. Klay Thompson had 20 points,

Warriors' guard Stephen Curry (30) prepares to shoot as Memphis Grizzlies guard Mike Conley (11) defends in the first half of Game 3.
AP Photo | Mark Humphrey

Memphis Grizzlies center Marc Gasol (33) reacts to contact from Warriors' center Festus Ezeli (31) in the second half.
AP Photo | Mark Humphrey

When the Warriors started to rally in the fourth quarter, Conley came through again. He made a 3-pointer to give the Grizzlies a 90-80 lead with 2:11 left, silencing the sea of golden yellow shirts for good.

Conley, who had three assists in 27 minutes, cramped up and went to the bench briefly in the final minutes.

By that point, his job was done.

Curry collected 19 points, six assists and five rebounds but had little help from backcourt teammate Klay Thompson, who was smothered by Allen's aggressive play. The Warriors had 20 turnovers and shot just 41.9 percent, including 23.1 percent from 3-point range. The Grizzlies had 13 steals.

"I thought we lost our poise tonight. We were in such a rush," Warriors coach Steve Kerr said.

Golden State had not lost at home since a 113-111 overtime defeat to Chicago on Jan. 27. The only other home loss came to San Antonio on Nov. 11.

"We're not going to overreact to one bad shooting night," Curry said."■

	1	2	3	4	T	Top Performers
Golden State	20	19	25	25	89	GS: K. Thompson 20 Pts, 8 Reb, 2 Ast, 1 Stl, 2 Blk
Memphis	23	32	24	20	99	Mem: Z. Randolph 22 Pts, 8 Reb, 3 Ast, 1 Stl

WARRIORS

STARTERS	MIN	FGM-A	3PM-A	FTM-A	OREB	DREB	REB	AST	STL	BLK	TO	PF	PTS
Harrison Barnes, SF	41	7-10	0-1	2-2	3	3	6	1	0	0	2	4	16
Draymond Green, SF	39	1-8	1-6	3-4	0	6	6	7	3	1	5	4	6
Andrew Bogut, C	22	1-4	0-0	0-0	4	4	8	2	0	1	0	4	2
Stephen Curry, PG	40	8-21	2-10	5-7	1	1	2	6	1	1	4	1	23
Klay Thompson, SG	37	8-13	3-6	1-4	2	6	8	2	1	2	3	5	20

BENCH	MIN	FGM-A	3PM-A	FTM-A	OREB	DREB	REB	AST	STL	BLK	TO	PF	PTS
Festus Ezeli, C	9	1-3	0-0	0-0	0	2	2	0	0	1	0	0	2
Marreese Speights, C	6	3-7	0-0	3-4	0	1	1	0	1	0	0	1	9
Shaun Livingston, PG	9	1-1	0-0	0-0	0	1	1	0	0	0	0	0	2
Leandro Barbosa, SG	11	0-0	0-0	0-0	0	0	0	1	1	0	3	3	0
Andre Iguodala, SG	28	2-7	0-3	5-7	0	5	5	1	0	1	0	1	9
David Lee, PF					DNP COACH'S DECISION								
James Michael McAdoo, SF					DNP COACH'S DECISION								
Justin Holiday, SG					DNP COACH'S DECISION								

TOTALS		FGM-A	3PM-A	FTM-A	OREB	DREB	REB	AST	STL	BLK	TO	PF	PTS
		32-74	6-26	19-28	10	29	39	20	7	7	17	23	89
		43.2%	23.1%	67.9%									

GRIZZLIES

STARTERS	MIN	FGM-A	3PM-A	FTM-A	OREB	DREB	REB	AST	STL	BLK	TO	PF	PTS
Zach Randolph, PF	37	9-15	0-1	4-4	2	6	8	3	1	0	3	3	22
Tony Allen, SF	33	4-8	0-0	0-0	0	5	5	2	4	1	5	3	8
Marc Gasol, C	36	6-17	0-0	9-10	3	12	15	2	1	0	1	6	21
Mike Conley, PG	32	3-10	2-6	3-4	0	0	0	5	0	0	1	2	11
Courtney Lee, SG	32	4-9	2-4	1-1	0	3	3	4	2	0	1	3	11

BENCH	MIN	FGM-A	3PM-A	FTM-A	OREB	DREB	REB	AST	STL	BLK	TO	PF	PTS
Jeff Green, SF	26	3-8	1-2	0-0	1	1	2	1	0	0	2	2	7
Kosta Koufos, C	15	4-4	0-0	0-0	4	2	6	1	0	1	0	2	8
Beno Udrih, PG	16	2-6	0-1	3-4	0	1	1	3	2	0	0	3	7
Vince Carter, SG	13	2-5	0-2	0-0	1	3	4	0	0	0	1	2	4
Jon Leuer, PF					DNP COACH'S DECISION								
JaMychal Green, PF					DNP COACH'S DECISION								
Nick Calathes, SG					DNP COACH'S DECISION								
Jordan Adams, SG					DNP COACH'S DECISION								

TOTALS		FGM-A	3PM-A	FTM-A	OREB	DREB	REB	AST	STL	BLK	TO	PF	PTS
		37-82	5-16	20-23	11	33	44	21	10	2	14	26	99
		45.1%	31.3%	87.0%									

Flagrant Fouls: None
Technical Fouls: PLAYERS: None – TEAMS: GOLDEN STATE (1) – COACHES: None
Officials: James Capers, Tony Brown, Monty McCutchen
Attendance: 18,119
Time of Game: 2:35

◄ Warriors' forward Harrison Barnes (40) shoots against Memphis Grizzlies center Marc Gasol (33) and forward Jeff Green (32). *AP Photo | Mark Humphrey*

WARRIORS 101 • GRIZZLIES 84

WARRIORS BOUNCE BACK TO TIE SERIES, 2-2

Steve Kerr challenged his Golden State Warriors to ratchet up the intensity to playoff level. With MVP Stephen Curry leading the way, they responded and looked like the team that cruised through the regular season.

Curry scored 21 of his 33 points by halftime, and the Warriors snapped their two-game skid Monday night by routing the Memphis Grizzlies 101-84 to tie the Western Conference semifinals at 2-2.

"Tonight we took a step towards understanding that sense of urgency and kind of competitiveness and physicality to the game," Kerr said. "It was probably our most competitive effort, definitely of the series, but probably of the playoffs just in terms of understanding you got to play every second."

The Warriors hadn't lost three straight games all season, and they never came close as they took back home-court advantage. Curry hadn't scored more than 23 points in a game in this series, and he nearly had that by halftime.

Draymond Green had 16 points and 10 rebounds for the Warriors while Klay Thompson had 15 points, Harrison Barnes 12 and Andre Iguodala 11.

"We set the tone the first quarter and kept the foot on the gas pedal the whole way, and that's how we play," Curry said.

Marc Gasol had 19 points and 10 rebounds for Memphis while Zach Randolph had 12 points and 11 rebounds. Mike Conley finished with 10 points and seven assists but was 4-of-15 from the field. Memphis pulled its starters with 3:00 left.

Warriors' forward Draymond Green (23) shoots over Memphis Grizzlies center Marc Gasol (33) in the first half of Game 4. *AP Photo | Mark Humphrey*

Warriors guard Stephen Curry (30) shoots a three point shot against Memphis Grizzlies guard Mike Conley (11). *AP Photo | Mark Humphrey*

Warriors' center Andrew Bogut (12) makes contact after blocking a shot by Memphis Grizzlies guard Vince Carter (15).
AP Photo | Mark Humphrey

"This series could have been close to over if we hadn't come out like we were supposed to tonight," Warriors center Andrew Bogut said. "You know it's never over until the end, but being down 3-1 going home is a pretty tough task, so 2-2 right now in a three-game series, we like our chances."

Memphis coach Dave Joerger had given his Grizzlies a history lesson reminding them of previous blown 2-1 leads in the postseason. It didn't help, as the Grizzlies lost their fourth straight Game 4, the third of those on their own court. They just didn't play with the same defensive intensity as the past two games.

"We lost our composure early in the first half, especially in the first quarter," Joerger said. "We needed to keep that closer in the first quarter. We

		1	2	3	4	T	Top Performers
Golden State		28	33	21	19	101	GS: S. Curry 33 Pts, 8 Reb, 5 Ast, 2 Stl
Memphis		20	24	20	20	84	Mem: M. Gasol 19 Pts, 10 Reb, 6 Ast, 1 Stl, 1 Blk

WARRIORS

STARTERS	MIN	FGM-A	3PM-A	FTM-A	OREB	DREB	REB	AST	STL	BLK	TO	PF	PTS
Harrison Barnes, SF	33	6-14	0-4	0-1	1	5	6	1	1	1	1	1	12
Draymond Green, SF	35	6-12	3-8	1-2	3	7	10	4	2	2	7	3	16
Andrew Bogut, C	30	2-3	0-0	0-0	2	7	9	4	3	3	4	5	4
Stephen Curry, PG	39	11-22	4-9	7-9	2	6	8	5	2	0	4	4	33
Klay Thompson, SG	40	6-15	3-6	0-0	0	2	2	2	2	1	3	2	15
BENCH	MIN	FGM-A	3PM-A	FTM-A	OREB	DREB	REB	AST	STL	BLK	TO	PF	PTS
David Lee, PF	15	2-5	0-0	1-2	1	0	1	1	0	1	0	3	5
James Michael McAdoo, SF	2	0-0	0-0	0-0	0	0	0	0	0	1	1	0	0
Festus Ezeli, C	2	0-0	0-0	0-0	0	2	2	0	0	0	0	0	0
Shaun Livingston, PG	16	0-1	0-0	2-2	0	2	2	2	0	1	1	1	2
Justin Holiday, SG	2	1-1	1-1	0-0	0	0	0	0	0	0	0	1	3
Brandon Rush, SG	2	0-1	0-0	0-0	0	0	0	0	0	0	0	1	0
Leandro Barbosa, SG	2	0-0	0-0	0-0	0	1	1	0	0	0	0	0	0
Andre Iguodala, SG	24	4-6	3-5	0-0	1	3	4	3	1	0	0	2	11
TOTALS		FGM-A	3PM-A	FTM-A	OREB	DREB	REB	AST	STL	BLK	TO	PF	PTS
		38-80	14-33	11-16	10	35	45	22	11	10	21	23	101
		47.5%	42.4%	68.8%									

GRIZZLIES

STARTERS	MIN	FGM-A	3PM-A	FTM-A	OREB	DREB	REB	AST	STL	BLK	TO	PF	PTS
Zach Randolph, PF	31	5-10	0-0	2-3	5	6	11	0	0	0	4	2	12
Tony Allen, SF	16	2-9	0-3	0-0	4	1	5	0	1	1	1	2	4
Marc Gasol, C	38	7-19	0-0	5-6	4	6	10	6	1	1	1	2	19
Mike Conley, PG	33	4-15	2-5	0-0	0	3	3	7	3	0	3	2	10
Courtney Lee, SG	30	3-7	0-3	0-0	1	2	3	3	1	0	2	0	6
BENCH	MIN	FGM-A	3PM-A	FTM-A	OREB	DREB	REB	AST	STL	BLK	TO	PF	PTS
Jon Leuer, PF	3	1-2	0-0	0-0	1	1	2	0	0	0	0	0	2
JaMychal Green, PF	3	0-0	0-0	2-2	0	1	1	0	1	1	0	0	2
Jeff Green, SF	34	4-8	1-2	3-4	0	3	3	3	1	1	3	3	12
Kosta Koufos, C	5	1-3	0-0	0-0	2	0	2	0	0	0	0	0	2
Beno Udrih, PG	17	2-5	0-2	0-0	0	1	1	3	0	0	1	2	4
Vince Carter, SG	24	4-9	1-3	1-1	0	7	7	0	0	0	1	4	10
Nick Calathes, SG	3	0-0	0-0	0-0	0	1	1	2	0	0	0	0	0
Jordan Adams, SG	2	0-1	0-0	1-2	0	0	0	0	0	0	0	0	1
TOTALS		FGM-A	3PM-A	FTM-A	OREB	DREB	REB	AST	STL	BLK	TO	PF	PTS
		33-88	4-18	14-18	17	32	49	24	8	4	16	17	84
		37.5%	22.2%	77.8%									

Flagrant Fouls: None
Technical Fouls: PLAYERS: None – TEAMS: None – COACHES: None
Officials: Pat Fraher, Mike Callahan, Tony Brothers
Attendance: 18,119
Time of Game: 2:20

had a chance there. Our offense really struggled tonight, and it put our defense in a bad way."

Green looked like the forward who got the most first-place votes for defensive player of the year. He teamed with Bogut and Barnes, making the night miserable for Randolph and Gasol with Bogut roving over to the paint while nominally defending Tony Allen. Green scored eight of Golden State's first 10 points.

Curry didn't take his first shot until 3:30 left in the first quarter, and he missed his first 3, along with a layup. He settled down and had seven points by the end of the period, including a 27-footer giving Golden State a 28-20 lead at the end of the frame. The Warriors outscored Memphis 33-24 in the second, taking a 61-44 halftime lead.■

WARRIORS 98 • GRIZZLIES 78

WARRIORS ROLL PAST GRIZZLIES

Down and out just days earlier, the Golden State Warriors suddenly look alive and well again.

Stephen Curry turned in an MVP-worthy performance, Klay Thompson snapped out of his shooting funk and the Warriors rolled past the Memphis Grizzlies 98-78 on Wednesday night to take a 3-2 lead in their Western Conference semifinal series.

"It's like wine," Warriors forward Draymond Green said about learning how to stop Memphis. "It gets better with time."

The Warriors turned up the league's top-rated defense and finally found their rhythm from long range.

Curry scored 18 points on six 3-pointers and added a career-playoff high six steals to go with seven rebounds and five assists. Thompson scored 21 points, and Harrison Barnes had 14 as the Warriors won their second straight game in impressive fashion.

"I think I said the first couple games, 'Our defense was good enough, but it wasn't championship defense,'" Warriors coach Steve Kerr said. "I was wrong. This is what it's going to take."

With defensive stopper Tony Allen sidelined with a left hamstring injury, the Grizzlies struggled to contain Golden State's streaky shooters. The Warriors made 14 of 30 shots from 3-point range, while Memphis made just four of 15 from long distance.

Marc Gasol had 18 points and 12 rebounds, and Zach Randolph had 13 points and 10 boards for a Grizzlies team suddenly on the brink of elimination. It was Memphis' lowest

Warriors' center Andrew Bogut, top, dunks against the Memphis Grizzlies during the first half of Game 5.
AP Photo | Ben Margot

Warriors' guard Stephen Curry, right, dribbles against Memphis Grizzlies forward Zach Randolph.
AP Photo | Ben Margot

point total in these playoffs.

Since going down 2-1 in the series, the top-seeded Warriors have rediscovered their regular-season form – swarming defense, pace-and-space offense and lots of long-range swishes.

And for the second time in three nights, Memphis had no answer for them.

"They're moving the ball. They're getting a lot more penetration. Everybody," said Grizzlies guard Mike Conley, who scored 13 points wearing a mask over his still-healing face. "When you do that, it's always tough to stop."

Curry carried the Warriors back from an early 13-point deficit, connecting on four 3-pointers to give Golden State a 26-25 lead at the end of the

first quarter. He motioned his hands wildly to the roaring, golden-yellow-shirt-wearing sellout crowd following the fourth make just before the buzzer, showing as much emotion as he ever has at home.

"You feel the energy of the crowd," Curry said. "It was a cool moment."

Added Kerr: "It was a miracle we had the lead after the first quarter."

The Warriors never gave it back, either.

Barnes helped build the momentum with several big plays in the second quarter, and Curry came back with another from long distance to put Golden State up 49-41 at the half.

The Warriors wore down the short-handed Grizzlies following the break with a fast-pace

Warriors' forward Andre
Iguodala goes in for a dunk.
AP Photo | Ben Margot

	1	2	3	4	T	Top Performers
Memphis	25	16	16	21	78	Mem: M. Gasol 18 Pts, 12 Reb, 6 Ast, 1 Stl, 1 Blk
Golden State	26	23	25	24	98	GS: S. Curry 18 Pts, 7 Reb, 5 Ast, 6 Stl

GRIZZLIES

STARTERS	MIN	FGM-A	3PM-A	FTM-A	OREB	DREB	REB	AST	STL	BLK	TO	PF	PTS
Zach Randolph, PF	34	6-12	1-1	0-0	5	5	10	1	1	0	4	2	13
Jeff Green, SF	28	5-13	0-2	0-0	0	4	4	1	0	0	1	1	10
Marc Gasol, C	36	8-22	0-0	2-2	2	10	12	6	1	1	2	3	18
Mike Conley, PG	33	5-10	0-2	3-3	0	0	0	5	3	0	2	3	13
Courtney Lee, SG	31	3-3	1-1	0-0	0	3	3	4	0	0	3	3	7

BENCH	MIN	FGM-A	3PM-A	FTM-A	OREB	DREB	REB	AST	STL	BLK	TO	PF	PTS
Jon Leuer, PF	3	1-2	0-0	0-0	1	1	2	0	0	0	0	0	2
JaMychal Green, PF	3	0-2	0-1	0-0	0	1	1	0	0	0	0	1	0
Kosta Koufos, C	14	0-4	0-0	1-2	1	1	2	0	0	0	1	1	1
Beno Udrih, PG	12	1-2	1-1	0-0	0	0	0	0	0	0	0	0	3
Russ Smith, PG	3	0-0	0-0	0-0	0	0	0	1	0	0	0	0	0
Vince Carter, SG	20	3-10	1-6	1-1	4	2	6	1	1	0	2	1	8
Nick Calathes, SG	19	0-2	0-1	0-0	0	2	2	2	2	0	1	2	0
Jordan Adams, SG	6	1-1	0-0	1-2	0	1	1	0	0	0	0	0	3

TOTALS		FGM-A	3PM-A	FTM-A	OREB	DREB	REB	AST	STL	BLK	TO	PF	PTS
		33-83	4-15	8-10	13	30	43	21	8	1	16	17	78
		39.8%	26.7%	80.0%									

WARRIORS

STARTERS	MIN	FGM-A	3PM-A	FTM-A	OREB	DREB	REB	AST	STL	BLK	TO	PF	PTS
Harrison Barnes, SF	33	4-8	3-5	3-5	2	1	3	1	0	1	5	0	14
Draymond Green, SF	31	3-9	0-5	1-1	2	3	5	9	1	0	1	4	7
Andrew Bogut, C	24	3-7	0-0	0-0	3	6	9	0	0	4	1	2	6
Stephen Curry, PG	33	6-16	6-13	0-0	2	5	7	5	6	0	5	0	18
Klay Thompson, SG	39	7-16	3-4	4-4	0	4	4	5	0	0	2	1	21

BENCH	MIN	FGM-A	3PM-A	FTM-A	OREB	DREB	REB	AST	STL	BLK	TO	PF	PTS
David Lee, PF	17	3-7	0-0	0-0	2	5	7	1	1	0	0	3	6
James Michael McAdoo, SF	3	2-2	0-0	0-0	0	1	1	0	0	0	0	0	4
Festus Ezeli, C	6	0-0	0-0	0-0	0	1	1	0	0	1	0	1	0
Shaun Livingston, PG	22	3-4	0-0	0-0	1	2	3	3	1	0	1	1	6
Justin Holiday, SG	3	0-1	0-0	0-0	0	0	0	0	0	0	0	0	0
Brandon Rush, SG	2	0-0	0-0	0-0	0	1	1	0	0	0	0	0	0
Leandro Barbosa, SG	3	0-1	0-0	0-0	0	0	0	1	0	0	0	0	0
Andre Iguodala, SG	25	7-10	2-3	0-0	2	1	3	3	0	0	1	1	16

TOTALS		FGM-A	3PM-A	FTM-A	OREB	DREB	REB	AST	STL	BLK	TO	PF	PTS
		38-81	14-30	8-10	14	30	44	28	9	6	16	13	98
		46.9%	46.7%	80.0%									

Flagrant Fouls: None
Technical Fouls: PLAYERS: 1 GOLDEN STATE (Iguodala 1) – TEAMS: MEMPHIS (1) – COACHES: None
Officials: Ed Malloy, Bill Spooner, Ken Mauer
Attendance: 19,596
Time of Game: 2:15

tempo that never relented.

They led 74-57 through three quarters and went ahead by 24 points early in the fourth on Thompson's four-point play, turning the game into the type of home wipeout that became routine in the regular season, when they rolled to a franchise-record 67 wins.

"That's our brand of basketball," Green said. "We got a couple of stops and all of a sudden the game started changing. It's tough for anybody to keep up with us in transition, but that has to start on the defensive end." ∎

WARRIORS 108 • GRIZZLIES 95

WARRIORS CLOSE OUT MEMPHIS

Golden State In First Western Conference Finals Since 1976

Stephen Curry practices tough shots every day. The MVP came up with a third-quarter buzzer-beater his coach calls the play of the game.

For Golden State, rank it among the Warriors' best shots in decades, and it helped put them in their first Western Conference finals since 1976.

Curry scored 32 points with that 62-footer among eight 3-pointers, and the Warriors beat the Memphis Grizzlies a third straight game, 108-95, on Friday.

"In a closeout game like that, that's a big turning point and the moment is magnified," said Curry, the NBA's MVP. "I made one in college like that. That's the last I made anywhere past half court and same kind of shot: loose ball, grab it, throw it up and knock it down."

First-year coach Steve Kerr called this a beautiful team win and a big moment for the Warriors. He said Curry was amazing, especially with that shot as the Grizzlies tried to make a run in the third quarter.

"It wasn't quite a closeout shot, but it was the play of the game," Kerr said.

The Warriors advanced with some of the best shooting in the NBA postseason since 1985, becoming the first team since that year to hit 14 or more 3s in three consecutive playoff games. Curry

Warriors' guard Stephen Curry (30) aims for the basket as Memphis Grizzlies guard Mike Conley defends.
AP Photo | Mark Humphrey

Memphis Grizzlies guard Vince Carter (15) defends Warriors' forward Harrison Barnes (40) during the second half.
AP Photo | Mark Humphrey

was 8-of-13 from beyond the arc as the Warriors knocked down their playoff-best 15 3-pointers.

Curry, who had 10 assists for his first double-double this postseason, hit the shot of the night after Andre Iguodala blocked Jeff Green's shot near midcourt. Curry grabbed the loose ball and beat the buzzer from the Grizzlies' 3-point line for a 76-68 lead.

Klay Thompson had 20 points for Golden State, and Draymond Green added 16, Harrison Barnes 13 and Shaun Livingston 10.

Curry finished the series with 25 3-pointers, one more than the Grizzlies managed as a team. When

he beat the buzzer with that long 3, he celebrated by bumping chests with Iguodala and David Lee. He then added 11 points in the fourth quarter to finish off the Grizzlies.

The Warriors outshot, outrebounded and simply did everything better than Memphis early, looking like the team that dominated the NBA regular season. Golden State led 32-19 by the end of the first quarter and Memphis had one more field goal (seven) than the Warriors had 3-pointers (six). The "Splash Brothers" outscored the Grizzlies by themselves, combining for 22 points.

But Curry and Thompson got plenty of help

Warriors' guard Stephen
Curry, back right, celebrates
a play with a teammate.
AP Photo | Mark Humphrey

KOUFOS
41

	1	2	3	4	T
Golden State	32	26	18	32	108
Memphis	19	30	19	27	95

Top Performers

GS: S. Curry 32 Pts, 6 Reb, 10 Ast

Mem: M. Gasol 21 Pts, 15 Reb, 4 Ast, 5 Blk

WARRIORS

STARTERS	MIN	FGM-A	3PM-A	FTM-A	OREB	DREB	REB	AST	STL	BLK	TO	PF	PTS
Harrison Barnes, SF	36	6-13	0-3	1-2	1	4	5	3	0	1	1	2	13
Draymond Green, SF	33	6-11	1-5	3-4	2	10	12	2	1	1	1	5	16
Andrew Bogut, C	24	2-3	0-0	0-0	0	3	3	2	0	3	1	6	4
Stephen Curry, PG	39	11-25	8-13	2-2	0	6	6	10	0	0	4	3	32
Klay Thompson, SG	37	7-13	3-5	3-3	2	6	8	3	0	0	3	2	20

BENCH	MIN	FGM-A	3PM-A	FTM-A	OREB	DREB	REB	AST	STL	BLK	TO	PF	PTS
David Lee, PF	14	1-3	0-0	0-0	2	3	5	0	0	1	0	2	2
Festus Ezeli, C	2	1-1	0-0	0-0	0	0	0	0	0	0	0	0	2
Shaun Livingston, PG	20	4-6	0-0	2-2	0	1	1	0	0	1	2	2	10
Leandro Barbosa, SG	4	0-0	0-0	0-0	0	1	1	0	0	0	0	1	0
Andre Iguodala, SG	30	3-6	3-6	0-1	0	6	6	7	0	1	0	1	9
James Michael McAdoo, SF		DNP COACH'S DECISION											
Justin Holiday, SG		DNP COACH'S DECISION											
Brandon Rush, SG		DNP COACH'S DECISION											

TOTALS		FGM-A	3PM-A	FTM-A	OREB	DREB	REB	AST	STL	BLK	TO	PF	PTS
		41-81	15-32	11-14	7	40	47	27	1	8	12	24	108
		50.6%	46.9%	78.6%									

GRIZZLIES

STARTERS	MIN	FGM-A	3PM-A	FTM-A	OREB	DREB	REB	AST	STL	BLK	TO	PF	PTS
Zach Randolph, PF	33	5-14	0-0	5-6	2	4	6	1	1	0	1	4	15
Tony Allen, SF	5	1-3	0-0	0-0	0	0	0	0	0	0	0	1	2
Marc Gasol, C	44	7-23	0-0	7-10	3	12	15	4	0	5	0	2	21
Mike Conley, PG	39	3-13	0-6	5-7	0	1	1	9	2	0	1	1	11
Courtney Lee, SG	38	5-12	2-4	0-0	0	2	2	3	1	0	0	2	12

BENCH	MIN	FGM-A	3PM-A	FTM-A	OREB	DREB	REB	AST	STL	BLK	TO	PF	PTS
JaMychal Green, PF	0	0-0	0-0	0-0	0	0	0	0	0	0	0	0	0
Jeff Green, SF	31	2-8	0-2	2-2	2	5	7	1	1	0	0	2	6
Kosta Koufos, C	14	4-5	0-0	0-0	4	4	8	1	1	0	0	0	8
Beno Udrih, PG	8	2-6	0-1	0-0	0	0	0	0	0	0	0	0	4
Vince Carter, SG	26	5-7	2-3	4-5	1	2	3	2	1	0	1	4	16
Nick Calathes, SG	1	0-0	0-0	0-0	0	1	1	0	0	0	0	0	0
Jon Leuer, PF		DNP COACH'S DECISION											
Jordan Adams, SG		DNP COACH'S DECISION											

TOTALS		FGM-A	3PM-A	FTM-A	OREB	DREB	REB	AST	STL	BLK	TO	PF	PTS
		34-91	4-16	23-30	12	31	43	21	7	5	3	16	95
		37.4%	25.0%	76.7%									

Flagrant Fouls: None
Technical Fouls: PLAYERS: None – TEAMS: None – COACHES: None
Officials: Zach Zarba, John Goble, Joe Crawford
Attendance: 18,119
Time of Game: 2:20

with teammates taking turns knocking down shots.

"I think what you see with their team is I think that they really grew up," Memphis coach Dave Joerger said. "They really grew through the battle of this series and matured to the point where I think that will help them, unfortunately, in the future being able to take the hits that they took, regroup and still win." ∎

COACH STEVE KERR

MODEST KERR A PERFECT FIT FOR WARRIORS

Golden State Warriors head coach Steve Kerr, led his team this season to the best record in professional basketball.

That's a remarkable feat for anyone, but especially for someone who has never coached before this season – even as an assistant.

Sports writer after sports writer has tried to explain Kerr's success as a first-time coach, as the Warriors barreled their way toward the NBA Finals. He had enormous talent to work with, particularly in the form of point guard Steph Curry, the league's MVP, and sharp shooting backcourt mate Klay Thompson. His predecessor is credited with building some of the key elements of this year's talented team. And he hired veteran assistants considered some of the best minds in basketball.

But for all those advantages, Kerr's biggest asset ultimately may be his own leadership skill. In analysis after analysis, a picture emerges of a coach who is humble, detailed and curious about the world. He gives his players opportunities, asks for their input and tries to keep the joy of the game. Most of all, his character remains calm under pressure yet still fiercely competitive.

"I try to approach coaching with the idea that I'm going to present myself totally, openly and honestly and communicate with everybody," Kerr said. "We have a group of guys that's pretty easy to coach so it really hasn't been much of an issue. But I do think because Steph is the best player, the rest of the guys follow his lead. The fact that he lets me get on him in film sessions, criticize him, and urge him to get better allows other guys to understand that they have to accept the same things."

"I respond best when a coach is able to get on me where he's raising his voice, yelling and whatever, because he expects greatness from me – especially when I'm not performing the way I'm supposed to," Curry said. "I like to have, obviously, a mutual respect, and a guy who can be as consistent as possible with his message. But if I need to be yelled at and refocused, I'm open to that and I usually respond well."

"That's maybe the most underrated aspect of Steph's game is his competitive desire," Kerr said. "The guy is an animal. Maybe you don't see it because he is slight of frame and he's a skill player, but his defense has been fantastic this year. His competitiveness – he hates to lose. And when he has a game that isn't up to his standards, you know he is going to bring it the next game. As a coach you love that." ■

Warriors' guard Stephen Curry (30) hugs head coach Steve Kerr during the second half of Game 6 of basketball's NBA Finals against the Cleveland Cavaliers. *AP Photo | Tony Dejak*

WARRIORS 110 • ROCKETS 106

CURRY LEADS WAY AS WARRIORS DOWN ROCKETS

Down big at home, the Golden State Warriors went small.

It turned out to make a huge difference.

Stephen Curry hit two free throws in the final seconds to finish with 34 points, and the Warriors rallied from a 16-point deficit in the second quarter to beat the Houston Rockets 110-106 on Tuesday night in Game 1 of the Western Conference finals.

With the Rockets seemingly ready to rout the home team, the Warriors used a smaller lineup featuring 6-foot-7 Draymond Green at center and closed the first half on a 21-4 run. Shaun Livingston scored 14 of his 18 points in the quarter, helping Golden State go ahead 58-55 at halftime.

The Warriors held off James Harden and Houston in the fourth quarter again behind their undersized lineup, which worked especially well after Rockets center Dwight Howard departed with a left knee injury.

"It really stretches people out," Warriors coach Steve Kerr said of his lineup full of shooters.

Warriors' guard Shaun Livingston (34) shoots over Houston Rockets center Clint Capela (15) during the first half. *AP Photo | Tony Avelar*

Warriors' guard Stephen Curry (30), launches a three-point shot over Houston Rockets center Clint Capela (15).
AP Photo | Tony Avelar

"Houston does the same thing. It was an interesting chess match, because they like to go small and we like to go small."

Harden, the runner-up to Curry in the MVP voting, nearly brought the Rockets back without Howard in the fourth. Harden finished with 28 points, 11 rebounds, 9 assists and 4 steals, but his late push fell short.

Harden, serenaded with chants of "Over-rated!" from Warriors fans, mixed in a series of step-back jumpers and driving layups to help Houston even

the score at 95-all midway through the fourth.

But the Warriors shut down Houston for long stretches, and Curry kept hitting shots to match Harden's brilliance. Curry connected on a 3-pointer and converted a layup to put Golden State up 108-97 with 2:01 remaining.

"It's entertaining basketball. We're both supposed to help our team win and do what we can to impact the game," said Curry.

The Rockets never relented, though, with Trevor Ariza making a 3-pointer that trimmed the

Warriors' center Festus Ezeli (31) blocks a shot attempt by Houston Rockets guard James Harden, bottom, during the second half.
AP Photo | Tony Avelar

	1	2	3	4	T
Houston	31	24	24	27	106
Golden State	24	34	26	26	110

Top Performers

Hou: J. Harden 28 Pts, 11 Reb, 9 Ast, 4 Stl

GS: S. Curry 34 Pts, 6 Reb, 5 Ast, 2 Stl

ROCKETS

STARTERS	MIN	FGM-A	3PM-A	FTM-A	OREB	DREB	REB	AST	STL	BLK	TO	PF	PTS
Josh Smith, SF	27	6-16	2-6	3-4	1	6	7	5	0	3	3	1	17
Trevor Ariza, SF	34	7-10	4-5	2-2	1	2	3	2	2	0	1	1	20
Dwight Howard, C	26	3-7	0-0	1-4	4	9	13	2	1	1	5	3	7
Jason Terry, SG	27	2-9	1-4	2-2	2	0	2	3	0	0	1	3	7
James Harden, SG	42	11-20	1-3	5-6	2	9	11	9	4	0	5	4	28

BENCH	MIN	FGM-A	3PM-A	FTM-A	OREB	DREB	REB	AST	STL	BLK	TO	PF	PTS
Terrence Jones, PF	26	2-10	0-2	1-4	3	1	4	1	0	1	0	0	5
Clint Capela, C	13	4-4	0-0	1-2	1	3	4	1	1	1	0	1	9
Pablo Prigioni, PG	15	2-3	0-1	0-0	0	1	1	4	0	0	0	1	4
Corey Brewer, SG	30	3-7	0-1	3-4	0	2	2	0	0	0	0	5	9
Kostas Papanikolaou, SF					DNP COACH'S DECISION								
Joey Dorsey, C					DNP COACH'S DECISION								
K.J. McDaniels, SG					DNP COACH'S DECISION								
Nick Johnson, SG					DNP COACH'S DECISION								

TOTALS		FGM-A	3PM-A	FTM-A	OREB	DREB	REB	AST	STL	BLK	TO	PF	PTS
		40-86	8-22	18-28	14	33	47	27	8	6	12	19	106
		46.5%	36.4%	64.3%									

WARRIORS

STARTERS	MIN	FGM-A	3PM-A	FTM-A	OREB	DREB	REB	AST	STL	BLK	TO	PF	PTS
Harrison Barnes, SF	33	6-12	2-6	0-0	1	0	1	1	2	0	2	3	14
Draymond Green, SF	43	6-13	0-3	1-2	4	8	12	8	2	1	3	2	13
Andrew Bogut, C	16	0-3	0-0	0-0	2	2	4	0	1	0	0	3	0
Stephen Curry, PG	39	13-22	6-11	2-3	0	6	6	5	2	0	1	3	34
Klay Thompson, SG	33	6-18	1-7	2-2	0	2	2	4	1	1	2	5	15

BENCH	MIN	FGM-A	3PM-A	FTM-A	OREB	DREB	REB	AST	STL	BLK	TO	PF	PTS
David Lee, PF	4	1-3	0-0	0-0	1	2	3	0	0	0	0	0	2
Festus Ezeli, C	11	2-4	0-0	2-4	2	2	4	1	0	1	2	1	6
Shaun Livingston, PG	29	6-8	0-0	6-6	2	5	7	3	1	0	2	2	18
Leandro Barbosa, SG	8	1-5	1-2	1-2	2	1	3	1	0	0	0	1	4
Andre Iguodala, SG	23	2-4	0-0	0-3	0	1	1	4	0	0	0	3	4
James Michael McAdoo, SF					DNP COACH'S DECISION								
Justin Holiday, SG					DNP COACH'S DECISION								
Brandon Rush, SG					DNP COACH'S DECISION								

TOTALS		FGM-A	3PM-A	FTM-A	OREB	DREB	REB	AST	STL	BLK	TO	PF	PTS
		43-92	10-29	14-22	14	29	43	27	9	3	12	23	110
		50.6%	46.9%	78.6%									

Flagrant Fouls: None

Technical Fouls: PLAYERS: None – TEAMS: None – COACHES: None

Officials: Sean Wright, Dan Crawford, Marc Davis

Attendance: 19,596

Time of Game: 2:28

Warriors' lead to 108-106 with 14.6 seconds to play.

Curry twice caught the inbounds pass, and the Rockets were forced to foul him both times. He hit both free throws to seal Golden State's win.

"When we go small, it's not necessarily small. We have guys out there that can guard multiple positions," Livingston said. "From there, it's just feeding off our crowd."

Curry added six rebounds and five assists, and Green had 13 points, 12 rebounds and eight assists to boost the Warriors when they needed it most.

"When you try to keep your big in against our small lineup," Green said. "It's rough."∎

WARRIORS 99 • ROCKETS 98

WARRIORS HANG ON FOR 2-0 LEAD

James Harden had Game 2 on his fingertips – and then he didn't.

Now the Golden State Warriors have the Western Conference finals in their grasp.

Stephen Curry scored 33 points before Harden lost the ball in the closing seconds to end a spectacular duel between the NBA MVP and runner-up, and the Warriors held off the Houston Rockets 99-98 on Thursday night to take a 2-0 lead in the series.

Harden rallied the Rockets from 17 points down in the second quarter and had a chance to finish off the comeback in the fourth. Instead, Klay Thompson and Curry trapped Harden, who lost the ball as time expired.

Harden fell to the floor and put his hands over his head as the Warriors celebrated on the court, the sellout crowd of 19,596 roared and golden-yellow confetti fell from the rafters.

"Kicking chairs," Harden said. "It's frustrating. It's frustrating to give the game away like that."

Harden had 38 points, 10 rebounds and nine assists, and Dwight Howard overcame a sprained left knee that slowed him down to finish with 19 points and

Warriors' guard Klay Thompson (11) dunks against Houston Rockets forward Terrence Jones. *AP Photo | Rick Bowmer*

Houston Rockets guard James Harden (13) loses the ball on the game's final play as Warriors' guards Stephen Curry, left, and Klay Thompson defend. *AP Photo | Rick Bowmer*

17 rebounds for a Rockets team headed home in a major hole.

Curry made five 3-pointers to go with six assists and three rebounds. He got a big boost from his teammates – notably Bogut, Draymond Green and Thompson – to regroup after the Warriors lost the big lead in the first half.

But the Warriors pulled ahead late in the fourth quarter because of Curry – with his shot and his passes.

Curry connected on a 3-pointer, then found Bogut under the rim for a layup that sent the 7-footer flexing his muscles and shouting to the roaring, yellow-shirt-wearing crowd. Bogut missed the ensuing free throw, but the Warriors led 96-89 with 2:25 left.

Harden brought Houston back, and the Rockets forced the Warriors into an eight-second, backcourt violation before Harden found Howard for an alley-oop that sliced Golden State's lead to 99-98 with 33 seconds remaining.

After a timeout, Harrison Barnes missed a difficult reverse layup contested by Howard as the shot clock nearly expired. Harden got the ball down the court, and McHale elected not to call timeout because his team had the Warriors scrambling and outmanned.

"I will take our best player heading downhill on a broken court any day of the week. That's where he feasts," McHale said.

Harden was defended by Thompson, and Curry came over near the 3-point line, where Harden lost

	1	2	3	4	T	Top Performers
Houston	28	27	20	23	98	Hou: J. Harden 38 Pts, 10 Reb, 9 Ast, 3 Stl, 1 Blk
Golden State	36	19	22	22	99	GS: S. Curry 33 Pts, 3 Reb, 6 Ast, 1 Stl

ROCKETS

STARTERS	MIN	FGM-A	3PM-A	FTM-A	OREB	DREB	REB	AST	STL	BLK	TO	PF	PTS
Josh Smith, SF	21	5-17	0-3	0-0	0	1	1	2	1	0	1	2	10
Trevor Ariza, SF	39	3-8	1-4	0-0	2	4	6	1	2	0	2	4	7
Dwight Howard, C	40	8-11	0-0	3-7	5	12	17	1	2	1	2	3	19
Jason Terry, SG	35	3-7	3-5	0-0	1	0	1	4	0	0	0	3	9
James Harden, SG	41	13-21	3-6	9-10	1	9	10	9	3	1	2	2	38

BENCH	MIN	FGM-A	3PM-A	FTM-A	OREB	DREB	REB	AST	STL	BLK	TO	PF	PTS
Terrence Jones, PF	26	6-12	0-1	0-0	1	1	2	1	1	3	2	1	12
Clint Capela, C	8	0-0	0-0	0-0	1	1	2	0	0	0	0	0	0
Pablo Prigioni, PG	7	0-2	0-2	0-0	0	0	0	1	1	0	0	1	0
Nick Johnson, SG	3	0-1	0-1	0-0	0	0	0	0	0	0	0	0	0
Corey Brewer, SG	19	1-5	0-1	1-2	0	0	0	1	0	0	1	2	3
Kostas Papanikolaou, SF				DNP COACH'S DECISION									
Joey Dorsey, C				DNP COACH'S DECISION									
K.J. McDaniels, SG				DNP COACH'S DECISION									

TOTALS		FGM-A	3PM-A	FTM-A	OREB	DREB	REB	AST	STL	BLK	TO	PF	PTS
		39-84	7-23	13-19	11	28	39	20	10	5	10	18	98
		46.4%	30.4%	68.4%									

WARRIORS

STARTERS	MIN	FGM-A	3PM-A	FTM-A	OREB	DREB	REB	AST	STL	BLK	TO	PF	PTS
Harrison Barnes, SF	28	3-8	1-2	0-0	2	2	4	4	2	0	0	0	7
Draymond Green, SF	39	3-9	1-3	5-7	0	8	8	7	1	1	4	4	12
Andrew Bogut, C	31	7-9	0-0	0-1	2	6	8	4	0	5	4	4	14
Stephen Curry, PG	37	13-21	5-11	2-3	0	3	3	6	1	0	6	2	33
Klay Thompson, SG	33	6-15	1-7	0-0	0	4	4	1	0	1	2	4	13

BENCH	MIN	FGM-A	3PM-A	FTM-A	OREB	DREB	REB	AST	STL	BLK	TO	PF	PTS
Festus Ezeli, C	12	1-3	0-0	0-0	2	4	6	0	0	1	0	2	2
Shaun Livingston, PG	14	4-4	0-0	0-0	1	3	4	0	0	0	0	1	8
Leandro Barbosa, SG	15	2-6	0-1	0-0	0	0	0	3	1	0	0	0	4
Andre Iguodala, SG	32	2-2	0-0	2-2	0	2	2	6	2	0	0	0	6
David Lee, PF				DNP COACH'S DECISION									
James Michael McAdoo, SF				DNP COACH'S DECISION									
Justin Holiday, SG				DNP COACH'S DECISION									
Brandon Rush, SG				DNP COACH'S DECISION									

TOTALS		FGM-A	3PM-A	FTM-A	OREB	DREB	REB	AST	STL	BLK	TO	PF	PTS
		41-77	8-24	9-13	7	32	39	31	7	8	16	17	99
		53.2%	33.3%	69.2%									

Flagrant Fouls: None
Technical Fouls: PLAYERS: None – TEAMS: HOUSTON (1), GOLDEN STATE (1) – COACHES: None
Officials: James Capers, John Goble, Monty McCutchen
Attendance: 19,596
Time of Game: 2:25

the ball. Time expired amid the scramble.

"You knew he probably wasn't going to pass," Curry said. "At that point, it's just don't let him get a shot off and try to be the hero."

The Warriors' bench ran onto the court in celebration. Harden lay on the floor until teammates helped him up.

"I just wanted to stay big and force a contested shot," Thompson said. "Steph made a great read with that double-team."

Thompson, Barnes and Leandro Barbosa took turns guarding Harden in the second half, when both teams struggled to contain the other's leading man.

"It's great competition," Warriors coach Steve Kerr said. "It's two teams that really want to get to the Finals."∎

WARRIORS 115 • ROCKETS 80

CURRY PUTS ON A SHOW – WARRIORS UP 3-0

Golden State coach Steve Kerr described Stephen Curry's performance Saturday night simply.

"Steph was Steph," Kerr said. Indeed.

The MVP did what he does best, using his extraordinary 3-point shooting to power a 40-point game and the Warriors made it look easy against Houston, beating the Rockets 115-80 to take a 3-0 lead in the Western Conference finals.

"He's had a brilliant season," Kerr said. "The shooting is hard to describe because I don't think we've ever seen anybody shoot the ball the way Steph does off the dribble, off the catch."

The Warriors won the first two games by just five points combined. There would be no such drama in this one, with Curry leading them to a 26-point advantage in the second quarter.

Now the baby-faced MVP has Golden State one victory away from its first trip to the NBA Finals since it won the 1975 title.

Curry was unstoppable, making seven 3-pointers to break the NBA record for most 3s in the playoffs in a season with 64.

MVP runner-up James Harden finished with 17 points behind 10-

Warriors' guard Stephen Curry (30) shoots as Houston Rockets guard Nick Johnson (3) defends. *AP Photo | David J. Phillip*

Houston Rockets center Dwight Howard (12) fouls Warriors' guard Stephen Curry (30) during the first half.
AP Photo | David J. Phillip

of-11 free throw shooting but made just three of 16 shots as the Rockets dropped three straight for the first time all season.

Curry had 37 points after three quarters and went to the bench for good with about 5½ minutes remaining after his seventh 3-pointer made it 103-73. He also had seven rebounds and five assists. Draymond Green and Klay Thompson added 17 points apiece for the Warriors.

The Warriors were in control of this one from the start and were up by 12 at the end of the first. But things got out of hand quickly when Curry heated up.

A pair of free throws by Harden cut the lead to nine points with about six minutes left in the quarter when Curry took over. He scored the next six points as part of a 16-5 run where he scored all but two of the Warriors points to push the lead to 54-34.

Curry broke the record for 3s in the playoffs on a long one from the top of the key that put Golden State up 49-32 about 4½ minutes before halftime. He did a little bit of everything in that span. There was the finger-roll layup, a bank shot, seven free throws and even a pair of rebounds to get Golden State rolling.

Houston couldn't do anything right on either end of the court for most of the second quarter and made just one field goal and missed six shots in the six minutes before halftime.

The Warriors led by 25 at halftime, and Houston opened the third quarter strong, using a 13-6 spurt

...... (31), dunks as Houston Rockets forward Terrence Jones (6), center Clint Capela (15) and guard James Harden (13) watch. *AP Photo | David J. Phillip*

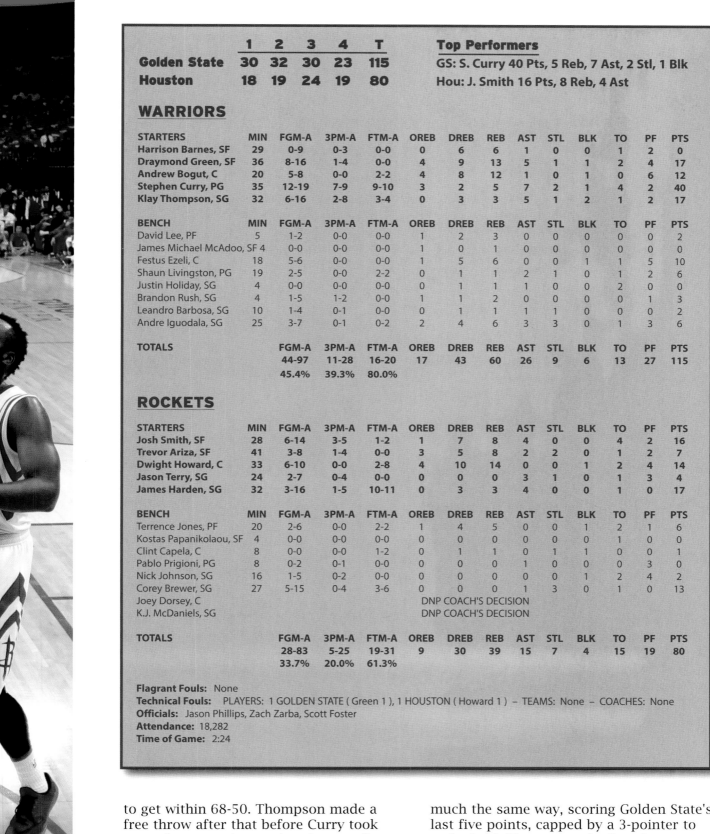

	1	2	3	4	T	Top Performers
Golden State	30	32	30	23	115	GS: S. Curry 40 Pts, 5 Reb, 7 Ast, 2 Stl, 1 Blk
Houston	18	19	24	19	80	Hou: J. Smith 16 Pts, 8 Reb, 4 Ast

WARRIORS

STARTERS	MIN	FGM-A	3PM-A	FTM-A	OREB	DREB	REB	AST	STL	BLK	TO	PF	PTS
Harrison Barnes, SF	29	0-9	0-3	0-0	0	6	6	1	0	0	1	2	0
Draymond Green, SF	36	8-16	1-4	0-0	4	9	13	5	1	1	2	4	17
Andrew Bogut, C	20	5-8	0-0	2-2	4	8	12	1	0	1	0	6	12
Stephen Curry, PG	35	12-19	7-9	9-10	3	2	5	7	2	1	4	2	40
Klay Thompson, SG	32	6-16	2-8	3-4	0	3	3	5	1	2	1	2	17

BENCH	MIN	FGM-A	3PM-A	FTM-A	OREB	DREB	REB	AST	STL	BLK	TO	PF	PTS
David Lee, PF	5	1-2	0-0	0-0	1	2	3	0	0	0	0	0	2
James Michael McAdoo, SF	4	0-0	0-0	0-0	1	0	1	0	0	0	0	0	0
Festus Ezeli, C	18	5-6	0-0	0-0	1	5	6	0	0	1	1	5	10
Shaun Livingston, PG	19	2-5	0-0	2-2	0	1	1	2	1	0	1	2	6
Justin Holiday, SG	4	0-0	0-0	0-0	0	1	1	1	0	0	2	0	0
Brandon Rush, SG	4	1-5	1-2	0-0	1	1	2	0	0	0	0	1	3
Leandro Barbosa, SG	10	1-4	0-1	0-0	0	1	1	1	1	0	0	0	2
Andre Iguodala, SG	25	3-7	0-1	0-2	2	4	6	3	3	0	1	3	6

TOTALS		FGM-A	3PM-A	FTM-A	OREB	DREB	REB	AST	STL	BLK	TO	PF	PTS
		44-97	11-28	16-20	17	43	60	26	9	6	13	27	115
		45.4%	39.3%	80.0%									

ROCKETS

STARTERS	MIN	FGM-A	3PM-A	FTM-A	OREB	DREB	REB	AST	STL	BLK	TO	PF	PTS
Josh Smith, SF	28	6-14	3-5	1-2	1	7	8	4	0	0	4	2	16
Trevor Ariza, SF	41	3-8	1-4	0-0	3	5	8	2	2	0	1	2	7
Dwight Howard, C	33	6-10	0-0	2-8	4	10	14	0	0	1	2	4	14
Jason Terry, SG	24	2-7	0-4	0-0	0	0	0	3	1	0	1	3	4
James Harden, SG	32	3-16	1-5	10-11	0	3	3	4	0	0	1	0	17

BENCH	MIN	FGM-A	3PM-A	FTM-A	OREB	DREB	REB	AST	STL	BLK	TO	PF	PTS
Terrence Jones, PF	20	2-6	0-0	2-2	1	4	5	0	0	1	2	1	6
Kostas Papanikolaou, SF	4	0-0	0-0	0-0	0	0	0	0	0	0	1	0	0
Clint Capela, C	8	0-0	0-0	1-2	0	1	1	0	1	1	0	0	1
Pablo Prigioni, PG	8	0-2	0-1	0-0	0	0	0	1	0	0	0	3	0
Nick Johnson, SG	16	1-5	0-2	0-0	0	0	0	0	0	1	2	4	2
Corey Brewer, SG	27	5-15	0-4	3-6	0	0	0	1	3	0	1	0	13
Joey Dorsey, C					DNP COACH'S DECISION								
K.J. McDaniels, SG					DNP COACH'S DECISION								

TOTALS		FGM-A	3PM-A	FTM-A	OREB	DREB	REB	AST	STL	BLK	TO	PF	PTS
		28-83	5-25	19-31	9	30	39	15	7	4	15	19	80
		33.7%	20.0%	61.3%									

Flagrant Fouls: None
Technical Fouls: PLAYERS: 1 GOLDEN STATE (Green 1), 1 HOUSTON (Howard 1) – TEAMS: None – COACHES: None
Officials: Jason Phillips, Zach Zarba, Scott Foster
Attendance: 18,282
Time of Game: 2:24

to get within 68-50. Thompson made a free throw after that before Curry took control once again, scoring the next five points, including a 3-pointer under heavy pressure, to push it to 75-50 midway through the third quarter.

He wrapped up the third quarter in much the same way, scoring Golden State's last five points, capped by a 3-pointer to make it 92-61 entering the fourth quarter.

Curry also became the first player in NBA history with five or more 3s in five straight postseason games.■

WARRIORS 115 • ROCKETS 128

HARDEN HELPS ROCKETS STAVE OFF ELIMINATION

James Harden was not happy after a poor performance in Houston's embarrassing loss to Golden State in Game 3.

Coach Kevin McHale told him the best thing to do was take that frustration out on the other team.

Harden did just that, scoring a playoff career-high 45 points as the Rockets led from start to finish to avoid elimination in the Western Conference finals with a 128-115 victory over the Warriors on Monday night.

The Rockets had a big lead after tying a playoff record with 45 points in the first quarter before Stephen Curry landed on his head in a nasty spill midway through the second and missed about 12 minutes.

His first field goal after returning came on a 3-pointer that got Golden State within six points with less than 8½ minutes remaining.

But Harden, who had 17 points in the fourth quarter, scored the next seven as part of 10 straight by Houston to push the lead to 114-98.

Klay Thompson had 24 points and Curry added 23 for Golden State.

But the Warriors couldn't put the Rockets away and will try again at home in Game 5 on Wednesday night.

The Warriors made 20 3-pointers and Houston had 17 to set an NBA record for most 3-pointers combined in a playoff game.

The Warriors used the Hack-A-Shaq technique on Josh Smith and got two 3-pointers from Curry to go on a 10-2 run to get within 10 with 4 minutes remaining.

A dunk by Andre Iguodala got them within eight with about 2 minutes left, but Harden answered with a 3-pointer to shut the door. Curry was injured after he jumped in the air as Trevor Ariza was about to go up for a shot.

Houston Rockets guard James Harden (13) shoots as Warriors' center Andrew Bogut (12) and forward Draymond Green (23) defend. *AP Photo | Pat Sullivan*

Warriors' forward Harrison
Barnes (40) dunks as
Houston Rockets center
Dwight Howard (12) defends.
AP Photo | David J. Phillip

Warriors guard Stephen Curry (30) topples over Houston Rockets forward Trevor Ariza (1).
AP Photo | David J. Phillip

Ariza saw him and stopped abruptly, causing Curry to be upended in midair when he crashed into Ariza's shoulder. His head hit the court and it propelled him up and back onto the floor, where he remained for several minutes.

Curry looked dazed as he was attended to before slowly getting up and walking off the court.

"I saw him kind of flip over ... Ariza," Golden State coach Steve Kerr said. "Obviously that's always scary." Ariza didn't realize who it was that sailed over him until the play was over.

"I was just trying to pump fake and get somebody off their feet," Ariza said. "I didn't know that he flipped over ... it wasn't intentional or anything like that."

	1	2	3	4	T	Top Performers
Golden State	22	37	25	31	115	GS: D. Green 21 Pts, 15 Reb, 4 Ast, 5 Blk
Houston	45	24	30	29	128	Hou: J. Harden 45 Pts, 9 Reb, 5 Ast, 2 Stl, 2 Blk

WARRIORS

STARTERS	MIN	FGM-A	3PM-A	FTM-A	OREB	DREB	REB	AST	STL	BLK	TO	PF	PTS
Harrison Barnes, SF	30	6-13	2-4	0-0	2	3	5	3	1	0	0	3	14
Draymond Green, SF	40	9-14	2-5	1-1	3	12	15	4	0	5	3	6	21
Andrew Bogut, C	21	0-1	0-0	0-2	0	8	8	4	0	1	3	4	0
Stephen Curry, PG	31	7-18	6-13	3-3	1	0	1	4	0	0	0	3	23
Klay Thompson, SG	38	9-21	6-13	0-0	1	2	3	2	2	0	4	5	24

BENCH	MIN	FGM-A	3PM-A	FTM-A	OREB	DREB	REB	AST	STL	BLK	TO	PF	PTS
David Lee, PF	3	0-0	0-0	0-0	0	1	1	0	1	0	1	1	0
Festus Ezeli, C	10	2-5	0-0	0-2	2	3	5	2	1	0	0	2	4
Shaun Livingston, PG	16	2-6	0-0	0-0	0	0	0	3	1	0	2	2	4
Leandro Barbosa, SG	24	5-10	2-5	0-0	0	2	2	2	0	0	0	2	12
Andre Iguodala, SG	26	4-9	2-6	3-5	1	6	7	2	3	3	2	1	13
James Michael McAdoo, SF		DNP COACH'S DECISION											
Justin Holiday, SG		DNP COACH'S DECISION											
Brandon Rush, SG		DNP COACH'S DECISION											

TOTALS		FGM-A	3PM-A	FTM-A	OREB	DREB	REB	AST	STL	BLK	TO	PF	PTS
		44-97	20-46	7-13	10	37	47	26	9	9	15	29	155
		45.4%	43.5%	53.8%									

ROCKETS

STARTERS	MIN	FGM-A	3PM-A	FTM-A	OREB	DREB	REB	AST	STL	BLK	TO	PF	PTS
Josh Smith, SF	28	6-14	3-5	1-2	1	7	8	4	0	0	4	2	16
Trevor Ariza, SF	41	3-8	1-4	0-0	3	5	8	2	2	0	1	2	7
Dwight Howard, C	33	6-10	0-0	2-8	4	10	14	0	0	1	2	4	14
Jason Terry, SG	24	2-7	0-4	0-0	0	0	0	3	1	0	1	3	4
James Harden, SG	32	3-16	1-5	10-11	0	3	3	4	0	0	1	0	17

BENCH	MIN	FGM-A	3PM-A	FTM-A	OREB	DREB	REB	AST	STL	BLK	TO	PF	PTS
Terrence Jones, PF	24	6-11	1-2	1-1	1	4	5	2	0	2	1	3	14
Clint Capela, C	4	1-1	0-0	2-4	0	1	1	0	0	0	0	0	4
Pablo Prigioni, PG	17	1-1	1-1	0-0	0	0	0	1	1	0	2	0	3
Corey Brewer, SG	22	0-4	0-1	1-2	0	2	2	2	0	1	0	1	1
Kostas Papanikolaou, SF		DNP COACH'S DECISION											
Joey Dorsey, C		DNP COACH'S DECISION											
K.J. McDaniels, SG		DNP COACH'S DECISION											
Nick Johnson, SG		DNP COACH'S DECISION											

TOTALS		FGM-A	3PM-A	FTM-A	OREB	DREB	REB	AST	STL	BLK	TO	PF	PTS
		43-76	17-32	25-43	4	42	46	22	8	10	16	16	128
		56.6%	53.1%	58.1%									

Flagrant Fouls: 1 HOUSTON (Howard 1)
Technical Fouls: PLAYERS: 1 GOLDEN STATE (Livingston 1), 1 HOUSTON (Jones 1) – TEAMS: None –
COACHES: 1 GOLDEN STATE (S Kerr 1)
Officials: Joe Crawford, Tom Washington, Mike Callahan
Attendance: 18,239
Time of Game: 2:32

Curry was called for a foul on the play and Ariza made both shots to extend Houston's lead to 57-36 with about six minutes until halftime. Thompson picked up the slack with Curry out, hitting four 3-pointers in a 23-9 run that get the Warriors within 66-59 with about 30 seconds left in the first half.

But Jason Terry hit a 3 as the shot clock expired to put Houston up 69-59 at halftime.

The Rockets led by nine when Curry re-entered the game midway through the third quarter. He shot an airball on his first shot after returning and his second try was blocked by Terrence Jones.■

WARRIORS 104 • ROCKETS 90

WARRIORS ADVANCE TO NBA FINALS FOR FIRST TIME SINCE 1975

After a generation of wishing and waiting, the Golden State Warriors have finally arrived again on basketball's biggest stage.

Stephen Curry had 26 points and eight rebounds, Harrison Barnes added 24 points, and the Warriors advanced to the NBA Finals for the first time in 40 years with a 104-90 victory over the Houston Rockets on Wednesday night.

"Why not us?" Curry said to a roaring, yellow shirt-wearing crowd after the Warriors received the Western Conference trophy from Alvin Attles, the coach of their last championship team in 1975.

"The Bay Area's been waiting for 40 years," Curry said later. "I think it's time."

The Warriors shook off a slow start and sweated out a shaky finish in Game 5 to close out the Rockets and set up a matchup with LeBron James and the Cleveland Cavaliers.

It was hardly the prettiest performance -- but one they'll savor nonetheless.

Yellow streamers and confetti fell from the rafters when the final buzzer sounded. The Warriors shared hugs and handshakes, and the crowd chanted, "M-V-P!" for Curry.

Curry said he had no lingering effects from his frightening fall in Game 4 that left him with a bruised head and right side. The NBA MVP wore a protective yellow sleeve on his right arm that he shed in the third quarter after shooting 4-for-12 and with the Warriors having led just 52-46 at halftime.

Things got tougher on Curry and the Warriors when backcourt mate Klay Thompson faked a shot that drew Trevor Ariza in the air early in the fourth quarter. Thompson absorbed Ariza's knee to the side of his head, sending him to the floor.

Warriors' guard Stephen Curry celebrates after Game 5.
AP Photo | Ben Margot

▲ Warriors' forward Harrison Barnes (40) shoots against Houston Rockets center Dwight Howard (12). *AP Photo | Ben Margot*

▶ Warriors' guard Klay Thompson, bottom, is injured in front of Houston Rockets guard James Harden (13) and forward Trevor Ariza (1). *AP Photo | Tony Avelar*

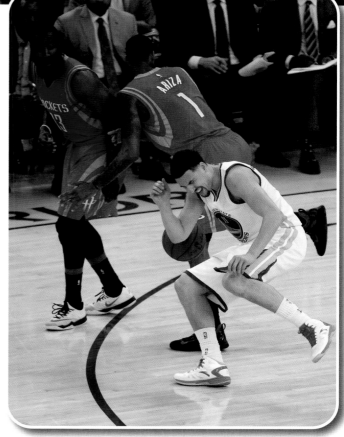

Thompson, who finished with 20 points, lay on the ground for a minute before walking to the locker room. He came back to the bench but had to receive stitches on his right ear.

The Warriors did just fine without him, starting the fourth on a 13-4 run and holding off Houston's last-ditch efforts on free throws. Barnes highlighted the decisive spurt with a dunk that gave Golden State an 87-72 lead with 7:10 remaining.

Now it's LeBron versus Curry.

King James versus the Baby-Faced Assassin.

The four-time NBA MVP versus the newly crowned MVP.

The hype has already started for two of the most popular and entertaining players in the world to take center stage for the championship, and it has a week to build even more before starting at Oracle Arena.

The conference title is the biggest accomplishment yet in what has been a rapid rise for

▲Golden State Warriors players celebrate after winning Game 5 of the NBA basketball Western Conference finals.
AP Photo | Tony Avelar

◄Warriors' forward David Lee, left, hugs coach Steve Kerr. *AP Photo | Tony Avelar*

	1	2	3	4	T	Top Performers
Houston	22	24	22	22	90	Hou: D. Howard 18 Pts, 16 Reb, 1 Ast, 2 Stl, 4 Blk
Golden State	17	35	22	30	104	GS: S. Curry 26 Pts, 8 Reb, 6 Ast, 5 Stl

ROCKETS

STARTERS	MIN	FGM-A	3PM-A	FTM-A	OREB	DREB	REB	AST	STL	BLK	TO	PF	PTS
Josh Smith, SF	21	3-14	2-7	3-6	1	3	4	1	0	2	0	2	11
Trevor Ariza, SF	44	5-9	1-3	4-4	2	4	6	4	2	0	1	5	15
Dwight Howard, C	42	5-13	0-0	8-13	3	13	16	1	2	4	4	3	18
Jason Terry, SG	39	6-13	2-8	2-2	0	2	2	3	1	0	2	3	16
James Harden, SG	43	2-11	0-3	10-13	2	4	6	5	3	0	12	5	14

BENCH	MIN	FGM-A	3PM-A	FTM-A	OREB	DREB	REB	AST	STL	BLK	TO	PF	PTS
Terrence Jones, PF	17	0-3	0-1	0-0	0	1	1	0	1	0	0	1	0
Clint Capela, C	3	0-0	0-0	0-0	1	0	1	0	1	0	0	1	0
Pablo Prigioni, PG	7	0-1	0-1	0-0	0	0	0	1	1	0	1	2	0
Corey Brewer, SG	24	5-10	0-1	6-6	1	2	3	1	1	0	0	4	16
Kostas Papanikolaou, SF				DNP COACH'S DECISION									
Joey Dorsey, C				DNP COACH'S DECISION									
K.J. McDaniels, SG				DNP COACH'S DECISION									
Nick Johnson, SG				DNP COACH'S DECISION									

TOTALS		FGM-A	3PM-A	FTM-A	OREB	DREB	REB	AST	STL	BLK	TO	PF	PTS
		26-74	5-24	33-44	10	29	39	16	12	6	20	26	90
		35.1%	20.8%	75.0%									

WARRIORS

STARTERS	MIN	FGM-A	3PM-A	FTM-A	OREB	DREB	REB	AST	STL	BLK	TO	PF	PTS
Harrison Barnes, SF	35	10-20	2-5	2-2	3	4	7	0	1	0	2	4	24
Draymond Green, SF	34	3-15	0-5	3-3	4	9	13	4	0	1	3	4	9
Andrew Bogut, C	19	0-1	0-0	0-0	5	9	14	1	0	2	1	2	0
Stephen Curry, PG	42	7-21	3-11	9-12	1	7	8	6	5	0	3	3	26
Klay Thompson, SG	22	8-14	4-6	0-0	0	1	1	4	1	0	0	5	20

BENCH	MIN	FGM-A	3PM-A	FTM-A	OREB	DREB	REB	AST	STL	BLK	TO	PF	PTS
David Lee, PF	0	0-0	0-0	0-0	0	0	0	0	0	0	0	0	0
Festus Ezeli, C	28	5-7	0-0	2-4	5	4	9	1	0	1	3	3	12
Shaun Livingston, PG	18	0-3	0-0	0-0	0	1	1	2	0	0	2	2	0
Leandro Barbosa, SG	11	1-2	0-1	5-6	0	2	2	1	0	0	0	4	7
Andre Iguodala, SG	30	3-8	0-1	0-4	1	3	4	6	3	0	2	3	6
James Michael McAdoo, SF				DNP COACH'S DECISION									
Justin Holiday, SG				DNP COACH'S DECISION									
Brandon Rush, SG				DNP COACH'S DECISION									

TOTALS		FGM-A	3PM-A	FTM-A	OREB	DREB	REB	AST	STL	BLK	TO	PF	PTS
		37-91	9-29	21-31	19	40	59	25	10	4	16	30	104
		40.7%	31.0%	67.7%									

Flagrant Fouls: None
Technical Fouls: PLAYERS: 1 HOUSTON (Howard 1), 1 GOLDEN STATE (Bogut 1) – TEAMS: None – COACHES: None
Officials: Ed Malloy, Ken Mauer, Tony Brothers
Attendance: 19,596
Time of Game: 2:44

a Warriors team that is beloved in the basketball-united Bay Area despite decades of futility.

General manager Bob Myers, the NBA executive of the year, has constructed a talented roster around Curry that has exceeded all expectations. And first-year coach Kerr blended it all together beautifully after Mark Jackson's messy firing last May.

"I always think of Pat Riley's great quote when you're coaching in the NBA, 'There's winning and there's misery.' And he's right," Kerr said. "It's more than relief. It's joy. Our players are feeling it. I know our fans are." ■

WARRIORS 108 • CAVALIERS 100

WARRIORS WIN IN OT – TAKE 1-0 LEAD

Stephen Curry had 26 points and eight assists, and the Golden State Warriors withstood a 44-point effort by LeBron James for a thrilling 108-100 overtime victory over Cleveland Cavaliers in Game 1 of the NBA Finals on Thursday night.

"It was just a classic five minutes that we needed to get that win," Curry said of the overtime.

In the Finals for the first time in 40 years, the Warriors gave their long-suffering fans quite a treat. They rallied from an early 14-point deficit, absorbed a personal Finals best point total from James and shut down Cleveland in the extra session.

James shot 18-of-38 from the field and had eight rebounds and six assists in 46 minutes. But the four-time MVP missed a long jumper at the end of regulation, and Cleveland missed its first eight shots of overtime -- and 12 straight going back to the fourth quarter.

Adding to the Cavs' frustration, point guard Kyrie Irving limped to the locker room after aggravating his troublesome left knee in overtime. He did not return.

There were 13 lead changes and 11 ties in a game tightly contested across the board. There was little

Cleveland Cavaliers forward LeBron James (23) shoots against Warriors' forward Andre Iguodala (9) during the first half. *AP Photo | Ben Margot*

Warriors center Andrew Bogut, foreground, grabs a rebound in front of Cleveland Cavaliers center Timofey Mozgov (20). *AP Photo | Ben Margot*

edge in shooting (Warriors 44.3 percent, Cavaliers 41.5 percent), rebounding (Warriors 48, Cavaliers 45) or assists (Warriors 24, Cavaliers 19).

The biggest difference might have been the benches. The Warriors' reserves outscored the Cavs' 34-9, with J.R. Smith the only Cleveland reserve to score -- and he was 3-of-13 from the field.

In the end, it came down to the biggest stars making plays -- or not.

James and Curry carried their clubs through the fourth quarter, trading scores and assists in a back-and-forth duel in front of a sellout crowd of 19,596 -- most wearing those blinding, golden-yellow shirts. Both also had a chance to win the game in regulation.

Curry, the current MVP, beat Irving off the dribble and moved in for the go-ahead layup. Instead, Irving blocked Curry from behind, Smith came up with the rebound and the Cavs called a timeout with 24.1 seconds left.

James, trying to end Cleveland's 51-year championship drought, dribbled down the clock and missed a contested jumper over Andre Iguodala just inside the left arc, and Iman Shumpert's desperation shot nearly went in at the buzzer, sending a collective sigh through the crowd.

The Cavs never came so close again.

Curry drew two deep shooting fouls at the start of overtime and made all four free throws, and Harrison Barnes hit a corner 3 just in front of the

Warriors forward Andre Iguodala (9) dunks against Cleveland Cavaliers center Tristan Thompson (13).
AP Photo | Eric Risberg

Cavs bench to give Golden State a 105-98 lead with 2:02 to play that had fans screaming at full throat.

Irving, who finished with 23 points, seven rebounds and six assists, limped to the bench trying to shake off his troublesome left leg after the play. He was replaced by Matthew Dellavedova.

The Warriors went ahead 108-98 on free throws with 1:16 to play. James' layup with 8.9 seconds left accounted for Cleveland's only points in overtime.

Klay Thompson, who wasn't cleared to play until Tuesday after suffering a concussion last week, scored 21 points and Iguodala added 15 points for a Warriors team that started slow but closed with a flurry.

"That's what we've been doing the whole year," Thompson said, "wearing down teams." ∎

Warriors' guard Stephen Curry (30) shoots the ball against Cleveland Cavaliers center Timofey Mozgov (20).
AP Photo | USA Today | Bob Donnan

	1	2	3	4	OT	T	Top Performers
Cleveland	29	22	22	25	2	100	Cle: L. James 44 Pts, 8 Reb, 6 Ast
Golden State	19	29	25	25	10	108	GS: S. Curry 26 Pts, 4 Reb, 8 Ast, 2 Stl

CAVALIERS

STARTERS	MIN	FGM-A	3PM-A	FTM-A	OREB	DREB	REB	AST	STL	BLK	TO	PF	PTS
LeBron James, SF	46	18-38	2-8	6-10	0	8	8	6	0	0	4	2	44
Timofey Mozgov, C	33	5-10	0-0	6-8	3	4	7	2	0	1	1	1	16
Tristan Thompson, C	47	1-4	0-0	0-0	6	9	15	1	1	1	2	3	2
Kyrie Irving, PG	44	10-22	2-8	1-1	2	5	7	6	4	2	1	5	23
Iman Shumpert, SG	34	2-6	2-4	0-0	1	1	2	0	4	1	2	2	6

BENCH	MIN	FGM-A	3PM-A	FTM-A	OREB	DREB	REB	AST	STL	BLK	TO	PF	PTS
James Jones, SF	17	0-1	0-1	0-0	0	1	1	1	1	0	1	4	0
Matthew Dellavedova, SG	9	0-0	0-0	0-0	1	0	1	3	0	0	0	1	0
J.R. Smith, SG	34	3-13	3-10	0-0	0	4	4	0	0	0	0	2	9
Kendrick Perkins, C					DNP COACH'S DECISION								
Brendan Haywood, C					DNP COACH'S DECISION								
Joe Harris, SG					DNP COACH'S DECISION								
Shawn Marion, SG					DNP COACH'S DECISION								
Mike Miller, SG					DNP COACH'S DECISION								

TOTALS		FGM-A	3PM-A	FTM-A	OREB	DREB	REB	AST	STL	BLK	TO	PF	PTS
		39-94	9-31	13-19	13	32	45	19	10	5	11	20	100
		41.5%	29.0%	68.4%									

WARRIORS

STARTERS	MIN	FGM-A	3PM-A	FTM-A	OREB	DREB	REB	AST	STL	BLK	TO	PF	PTS
Harrison Barnes, SF	39	4-9	3-5	0-0	2	4	6	1	1	0	0	2	11
Draymond Green, SF	39	4-13	0-3	4-4	2	4	6	3	2	0	1	5	12
Andrew Bogut, C	28	2-5	0-0	0-0	3	4	7	3	1	2	1	2	4
Stephen Curry, PG	43	10-20	2-6	4-4	0	4	4	8	2	0	4	1	26
Klay Thompson, SG	39	5-14	3-9	8-8	1	5	6	1	1	2	1	1	21

BENCH	MIN	FGM-A	3PM-A	FTM-A	OREB	DREB	REB	AST	STL	BLK	TO	PF	PTS
Festus Ezeli, C	12	1-1	0-0	3-4	0	5	5	1	0	0	1	1	5
Marreese Speights, C	9	4-8	0-0	0-0	2	1	3	1	0	0	1	2	8
Shaun Livingston, PG	16	2-6	0-0	0-0	1	4	5	3	0	0	0	0	4
Leandro Barbosa, SG	9	1-4	0-1	0-0	0	3	3	1	0	0	2	0	2
Andre Iguodala, SG	32	6-8	2-3	1-2	0	3	3	2	1	1	1	2	15
David Lee, PF					DNP COACH'S DECISION								
James Michael McAdoo, SG					DNP COACH'S DECISION								
Justin Holiday, SG					DNP COACH'S DECISION								

TOTALS		FGM-A	3PM-A	FTM-A	OREB	DREB	REB	AST	STL	BLK	TO	PF	PTS
		39-88	10-27	20-22	11	37	48	24	8	5	12	16	108
		44.3%	37.0%	90.9%									

Flagrant Fouls: None
Technical Fouls: PLAYERS: None – TEAMS: GOLDEN STATE (1) – COACHES: None
Officials: Jason Phillips, James Capers, Monty McCutchen
Attendance: 19,596
Time of Game: 2:41

◄ **Cleveland Cavaliers guard Kyrie Irving (2) tries to control the ball next to Golden State Warriors guard Klay Thompson during overtime. Irving left the game with an injury right after this play.**
AP Photo | Ben Margot

WARRIORS 93 • CAVALIERS 95

LEBRON JAMES' TRIPLE-DOUBLE HELPS CAVS EVEN FINALS

The final buzzer sounded, and LeBron James wasn't done.

As fans filed out of the quieting arena, James grabbed the ball and spiked it with all his might. He flexed his arms and pounded his chest, letting out a roar that echoed from California to Cleveland.

James turned in a triple-double to remember, Matthew Dellavedova made the go-ahead free throws in overtime and the Cavaliers overcame a fourth-quarter collapse to outlast the Golden State Warriors 95-93 on Sunday night to even the NBA Finals at a game apiece.

James finished with 39 points, 16 rebounds and 11 assists in 50 minutes, carrying Cleveland's depleted roster to victory on the NBA's toughest home floor. The Warriors had been 47-3 at ear-piercing Oracle Arena.

It was the second straight overtime game and one the Cavs never should've let happen.

Stephen Curry had a horrific shooting performance but converted the tying layup for the Warriors late in regulation. The MVP also put Golden State in front 93-92 on free throws with 29.5 seconds left in overtime.

Then, Draymond Green met James at the rim to block his left-handed layup, but the Cavs retained possession. After James Jones missed a 3-pointer, Dellavedova grabbed the rebound and was fouled.

Dellavedova made both to put Cleveland up with 10.1 seconds to play. Curry air-balled a jumper contested by Dellavedova, James got the rebound and hit one of two free throws with 4.4 seconds left.

After James made his free throw, Curry, without a timeout, raced up court and tried to pass ahead to Klay Thompson. But Iman Shumpert batted the ball away to seal the Cavs' win.

It was a pivotal point for the Cavs, who won their first Finals game in franchise history. Cleveland was staring at a major deficit again. Teams with a 2-0 lead have gone on to win 28 of 31 series.

Now that's one thing the Cavs won't have to overcome.

Curry scored 19 points and shot 5-of-23 from the floor, including 2-of-15 from 3-point range, and had six turnovers.

"Shots I normally make I knew as soon as they left my hand that they were off. That doesn't usually happen," Curry said. "Mechanically, I don't know if there is an explanation for it. Just didn't have a rhythm and didn't find one the whole game."

Golden State Warriors guard Klay Thompson (11) shoots against the Cleveland Cavaliers.
AP Photo | Eric Risberg

Cleveland Cavaliers forward LeBron James (23) shoots against Golden State Warriors guard Shaun Livingston (34) and center Festus Ezeli during the first half. *AP Photo | Ben Margot*

Thompson tried to pick up the backcourt slack, scoring 34 points. But the Warriors went 8-for-35 from long range and shot 39.8 percent overall.

The Cavs, who shot 32.2 percent, outrebounded the Warriors 55 to 45. It was the lowest shooting percentage for a winning team in the playoffs since at least 1984-85.

"It's the grit squad right now," James said. "If you expect us to play sexy, cute basketball, that's not us right now. Everything is tough, and it has to be that for rest of series."

"This is the Finals. It's hard. It's supposed to be hard," Warriors coach Steve Kerr said. "We had a tough night. So you have to move on. You've got to learn from it and get better, and that's what we're going to do." ∎

Warriors' forward Draymond Green, right, blocks a shot attempt by Cleveland Cavaliers forward LeBron James. *AP Photo | USA Today | Ben Margot*

	1	2	3	4	OT	T	Top Performers
Cleveland	20	27	15	25	8	95	Cle: L. James 39 Pts, 16 Reb, 11 Ast, 1 Stl, 1 Blk
Golden State	20	25	14	28	6	93	GS: K. Thompson 34 Pts, 5 Reb, 2 Ast, 2 Stl, 1 Blk

CAVALIERS

STARTERS	MIN	FGM-A	3PM-A	FTM-A	OREB	DREB	REB	AST	STL	BLK	TO	PF	PTS
LeBron James, SF	50	11-35	3-6	14-18	4	12	16	11	1	1	3	3	39
Timofey Mozgov, C	29	5-8	0-0	7-12	2	9	11	0	0	0	2	1	17
Tristan Thompson, C	39	0-5	0-0	2-4	7	7	14	0	1	1	0	5	2
Iman Shumpert, SG	36	2-11	1-5	2-2	0	3	3	1	3	1	0	1	7
Matthew Dellavedova, SG	42	3-10	1-6	2-2	1	4	5	1	3	0	6	3	9

BENCH	MIN	FGM-A	3PM-A	FTM-A	OREB	DREB	REB	AST	STL	BLK	TO	PF	PTS
James Jones, SF	23	3-7	2-4	0-0	0	1	1	1	2	0	0	4	8
Mike Miller, SG	6	0-1	0-1	0-0	0	1	1	0	0	0	0	1	0
J.R. Smith, SG	38	5-13	2-5	1-2	0	4	4	0	1	0	2	6	13
Brendan Haywood, C					DNP COACH'S DECISION								
Kendrick Perkins, C					DNP COACH'S DECISION								
Kyrie Irving, PG					DNP KNEE INJURY								
Joe Harris, SG					DNP COACH'S DECISION								
Shawn Marion, SG					DNP COACH'S DECISION								

TOTALS		FGM-A	3PM-A	FTM-A	OREB	DREB	REB	AST	STL	BLK	TO	PF	PTS
		29-90	9-27	28-40	14	41	55	14	11	3	13	24	95
		32.2%	33.3%	70.0%									

WARRIORS

STARTERS	MIN	FGM-A	3PM-A	FTM-A	OREB	DREB	REB	AST	STL	BLK	TO	PF	PTS
Harrison Barnes, SF	41	5-10	0-4	1-1	4	2	6	0	1	0	0	5	11
Draymond Green, SF	43	2-7	0-1	6-6	2	8	10	2	5	4	4	5	10
Andrew Bogut, C	25	0-1	0-0	2-4	1	9	10	1	0	2	2	4	2
Stephen Curry, PG	42	5-23	2-15	7-8	0	6	6	5	0	0	6	4	19
Klay Thompson, SG	46	14-28	4-12	2-3	0	5	5	2	2	1	0	4	34

BENCH	MIN	FGM-A	3PM-A	FTM-A	OREB	DREB	REB	AST	STL	BLK	TO	PF	PTS
Festus Ezeli, C	6	1-2	0-0	0-0	0	0	0	0	0	0	0	3	2
Marreese Speights, C	5	0-3	0-0	0-0	0	0	0	1	0	0	0	0	0
Shaun Livingston, PG	14	1-2	0-0	1-2	0	1	1	1	1	0	2	0	3
Leandro Barbosa, SG	6	2-2	1-1	0-0	1	0	1	0	0	0	0	1	5
Andre Iguodala, SG	36	3-5	1-2	0-1	2	4	6	5	1	0	4	5	7
David Lee, PF					DNP COACH'S DECISION								
James Michael McAdoo, SG					DNP COACH'S DECISION								
Justin Holiday, SG					DNP COACH'S DECISION								

TOTALS		FGM-A	3PM-A	FTM-A	OREB	DREB	REB	AST	STL	BLK	TO	PF	PTS
		33-83	8-35	19-25	10	35	45	16	11	7	18	31	93
		39.8%	22.9%	76.0%									

Flagrant Fouls: None
Technical Fouls: PLAYERS: 1 CLEVELAND (Smith 1), 1 GOLDEN STATE (Green 1) – TEAMS: None – COACHES: None
Officials: Zach Zarba, Scott Foster, Tony Brothers
Attendance: 19,596
Time of Game: 3:07

◄Cleveland Cavaliers forward LeBron James
(23) celebrates after end of the overtime period
of Game 2. *AP Photo | Ben Margot*

WARRIORS 91 • CAVALIERS 96

CAVS DEFENSE LEADS WAY – TAKE 2-1 LEAD IN FINALS

Pushed by a crowd howling to see Cleveland's 51-year title drought end, LeBron James scored 40 points, his new sidekick Matthew Dellavedova added 20 and the Cavaliers survived Golden State's furious fourth-quarter comeback led by Stephen Curry for a 96-91 win over the Warriors to take a 2-1 lead in the NBA Finals.

James added 12 rebounds and eight assists in 46 minutes, his third stellar performance in his fifth straight Finals. The Cavs, who won Game 2 at Golden State for their first ever Finals win, got their first at Quicken Loans Arena, which shook from start to finish.

Cleveland nearly threw Game 3 away. The Cavs, who led 92-83 with 51 seconds left, had to withstand a scoring flurry by Curry.

The league's MVP finally found his shooting touch in the fourth quarter, scoring 17 points as the Warriors, who trailed by 20 in the third, refused to go away. Golden State got a huge lift from reserve David Lee, but they rode Curry, who made five 3-pointers -- his last with 18.9 seconds to pull the Warriors within 94-91.

Cleveland then caught a break when referee Danny Crawford blew an inadvertent whistle with 17.5 seconds to go after Golden State appeared to force a turnover. The officials, who have come under scrutiny for several missed calls in the series, then reviewed the play and it was clear that Klay Thompson was out of bounds when he made contact with the ball that Dellavedova was holding in his hands.

James was fouled and made two free throws with 16.8 seconds left. On Golden State's last possession, Andre Iguodala appeared to get fouled on a 3-point attempt and the Cavs pulled down the rebound to close out a win that nearly slipped away.

"We're a young group," James said, "and like I told the group, 'It's OK.' We haven't been in a lot of these situations, if any, with this group."

Curry finished with 27 points but had three turnovers in the final minute. Iguodala scored 15, Klay Thompson, 14 and Lee, who didn't play in Games 1 or 2, had 11.

Despite the loss, Curry feels he's now in a rhythm.

"I think I found something when it comes to how I'm going to be able to attack their pick-and-rolls," Curry said. "I'll keep that in the memory bank going into Game 4."

After two overtime games in Oakland, Game 3 didn't have quite the same last-second drama, but it didn't lack any intensity as players were sprawled on the floor fighting for loose balls like the Browns and 49ers scrambling for fumbles.

The Cavs seemed to take control in the third, building their 20-point lead with a breathtaking 12-0 run that included 3-

Warriors' guard Stephen Curry (30) fouls Cleveland Cavaliers guard Matthew Dellavedova (8) as he shoots. *AP Photo | Tony Dejak*

Cleveland Cavaliers forward LeBron James (23) drives on Warriors' guard Andre Iguodala (9).
AP Photo | Tony Dejak

▲Cleveland Cavaliers forward LeBron
James (23) attempts to draw the charge
from Warriors' forward David Lee (10).
AP Photo | Paul Sancya

Cleveland Cavaliers guard Matthew Dellavedova (8) shoots in front of Warriors' guard Klay Thompson (11) during the second half. *AP Photo | Paul Sancya*

	1	2	3	4	T	Top Performers
Golden State	20	17	18	36	91	GS: S. Curry 27 Pts, 6 Reb, 6 Ast, 3 Stl, 1 Blk
Cleveland	24	20	28	24	96	Cle: L. James 40 Pts, 12 Reb, 8 Ast, 4 Stl, 2 Blk

WARRIORS

STARTERS	MIN	FGM-A	3PM-A	FTM-A	OREB	DREB	REB	AST	STL	BLK	TO	PF	PTS
Harrison Barnes, SF	19	0-8	0-1	0-0	3	0	3	0	0	0	3	2	0
Draymond Green, SF	30	2-10	1-4	2-3	3	4	7	3	1	0	1	4	7
Andrew Bogut, C	17	2-3	0-0	0-0	1	5	6	1	0	1	0	2	4
Stephen Curry, PG	44	10-20	7-13	0-0	2	4	6	6	3	1	6	2	27
Klay Thompson, SG	39	6-16	2-7	0-0	1	4	5	1	0	1	1	4	14
BENCH	**MIN**	**FGM-A**	**3PM-A**	**FTM-A**	**OREB**	**DREB**	**REB**	**AST**	**STL**	**BLK**	**TO**	**PF**	**PTS**
David Lee, PF	13	4-4	0-0	3-5	2	2	4	2	1	0	0	5	11
Festus Ezeli, C	18	2-6	0-0	1-2	3	4	7	1	0	2	2	1	5
Shaun Livingston, PG	13	2-4	0-1	0-0	2	0	2	2	0	0	1	3	4
Leandro Barbosa, SG	11	2-7	0-0	0-0	0	1	1	0	1	1	0	1	4
Andre Iguodala, SG	36	6-12	2-8	1-2	1	4	5	5	0	1	0	1	15
James Michael McAdoo, SG				DNP COACH'S DECISION									
Marreese Speights, C				DNP COACH'S DECISION									
Justin Holiday, SG				DNP COACH'S DECISION									
TOTALS		**FGM-A**	**3PM-A**	**FTM-A**	**OREB**	**DREB**	**REB**	**AST**	**STL**	**BLK**	**TO**	**PF**	**PTS**
		36-90	12-34	7-12	18	28	46	21	6	7	14	25	91
		40.0%	35.3%	58.3%									

CAVALIERS

STARTERS	MIN	FGM-A	3PM-A	FTM-A	OREB	DREB	REB	AST	STL	BLK	TO	PF	PTS
LeBron James, SF	46	14-34	2-6	10-12	1	11	12	8	4	2	4	1	40
Timofey Mozgov, C	32	3-6	0-0	0-0	0	5	5	1	1	4	4	3	6
Tristan Thompson, C	44	4-6	0-0	2-4	4	9	13	1	0	0	1	1	10
Iman Shumpert, SG	32	1-2	1-2	0-2	0	3	3	0	3	0	2	4	3
Matthew Dellavedova, SG	39	7-17	2-6	4-5	1	4	5	4	0	0	2	3	20
BENCH	**MIN**	**FGM-A**	**3PM-A**	**FTM-A**	**OREB**	**DREB**	**REB**	**AST**	**STL**	**BLK**	**TO**	**PF**	**PTS**
James Jones, SF	10	2-2	2-2	1-1	0	1	1	0	0	0	1	3	7
Mike Miller, SG	5	0-0	0-0	0-0	0	0	0	0	1	0	0	0	0
J.R. Smith, SG	32	4-9	2-5	0-0	0	4	4	1	0	2	0	1	10
Brendan Haywood, C				DNP COACH'S DECISION									
Kendrick Perkins, C				DNP COACH'S DECISION									
Kyrie Irving, PG				DNP KNEE INJURY									
Joe Harris, SG				DNP COACH'S DECISION									
Shawn Marion, SG				DNP COACH'S DECISION									
TOTALS		**FGM-A**	**3PM-A**	**FTM-A**	**OREB**	**DREB**	**REB**	**AST**	**STL**	**BLK**	**TO**	**PF**	**PTS**
		35-76	9-21	17-24	6	37	43	15	9	8	14	16	96
		46.1%	42.9%	70.8%									

Flagrant Fouls: None
Technical Fouls: PLAYERS: None – TEAMS: None – COACHES: None
Officials: Ed Malloy, Dan Crawford, Marc Davis
Attendance: 20,562
Time of Game: 2:37

pointers by James and J.R. Smith. Curry ended the spurt with a 3 and the Warriors opened the final period with a 13-2 blast to make it 74-68.

Curry, who went just 2-of-15 on 3s in Game 2, hit a couple did-he-really-just-do-that 3s in the fourth that have made him one of the game's most captivating players before the Warriors ran out of time.

Still, they're confident they can come back again.

"I'm telling you that right now," Thompson said, "if we get our offense back, which we will, we're going to win this series." ■

WARRIORS 103 • CAVALIERS 82

LINEUP CHANGE HELPS WARRIORS SQUARE SERIES 2-2

Stephen Curry shook off Iman Shumpert with a dribble, stepped back behind the line and splashed a 3-pointer that seemed to submerge a mute button on rocking and rolling Quicken Loans Arena.

Curry clenched both fists, slapped his chest and yelled, "C'mon!"

At last, this was the MVP and these were the Golden State Warriors – so deep, so deadly.

Curry and Andre Iguodala scored 22 points apiece and the Warriors, showing why they were the league's best team all season, squared the NBA Finals at 2-2 with a 103-82 victory over the Cleveland Cavaliers.

"Tonight we came in with the mentality that we had to win this game," Curry said.

So they did. These guys are California cool.

"We played desperate out there, man," Klay Thompson said. "We played real hungry. It was just awesome to come out here and impose our will on both sides of the ball and play our brand of basketball. That's what's been winning us games all year."

LeBron James scored 20 points – 21 under his average in the series – with 12 rebounds and eight assists, but Cleveland's megastar, who needed stitches to close a cut on his head sustained when he banged it into a camera in the first half, didn't score in the fourth quarter and couldn't do enough for the undermanned Cavaliers.

Timofey Mozgov led Cleveland with 28 points and guard Matthew Dellavedova, again

Golden State Warriors guard Andre Iguodala (9) goes up for a dunk over Cleveland Cavaliers forward James Jones (1) during the first half.
AP Photo | Paul Sancya

Warriors' forward Draymond Green, left, steals the ball from Cleveland Cavaliers guard Matthew Dellavedova (8).
AP Photo | Tony Dejak

battling leg cramps after a hospital stay for dehydration, had 10.

The Cavs looked tired and played tired. But they're not done yet.

Building off a strong fourth quarter in Game 3 that gave them confidence, the Warriors showed a sense of urgency from the outset and took it to the Cavs. Iguodala, who played so well coming off the bench in the first three games, made his first start this season and made coach Steve Kerr's decision look brilliant.

Known for his defense, Iguodala drained four 3-pointers, kept James in check and Curry made four

3s as well, including a deep dagger in the fourth over Iman Shumpert to end any thought the Cavs had of a comeback.

Iguodala said he tried to make things tough on James, who went 7-of-22 from the field and 5-of-10 from the free throw line.

"Make him work as hard as possible," Iguodala said of his plan on James. "Make him take tough shots. You look at his strengths, you look at his weaknesses, and you try to take him out of his comfort zone. Sounds easier said than done, but we all have a lot of talent and when we go out there we want to make our stamp on the game."

Cleveland Cavaliers forward LeBron James (23) is hit by Golden State Warriors center Andrew Bogut. *AP Photo | Paul Sancya*

▼Cleveland Cavaliers forward LeBron James (23) holds a towel to his head after being knocked into the fans. *AP Photo | Paul Sancya*

Warriors' forward Harrison Barnes (40) goes up for a dunk against the Cleveland Cavaliers.
AP Photo | Larry W. Smith

	1	2	3	4	T	Top Performers
Golden State	31	23	22	27	103	GS: D. Green 17 Pts, 7 Reb, 6 Ast, 2 Stl, 1 Blk
Cleveland	24	18	28	12	82	Cle: T. Mozgov 28 Pts, 10 Reb, 1 Ast, 1 Stl

WARRIORS

STARTERS	MIN	FGM-A	3PM-A	FTM-A	OREB	DREB	REB	AST	STL	BLK	TO	PF	PTS
Harrison Barnes, SF	33	4-9	2-5	4-4	3	5	8	0	0	2	0	2	14
Draymond Green, SF	32	6-11	1-3	4-7	0	7	7	6	2	1	0	5	17
Stephen Curry, PG	41	8-17	4-7	2-2	0	2	2	7	1	0	4	1	22
Andre Iquodala, SG	39	8-15	4-9	2-2	1	7	8	0	1	0	1	4	22
Klay Thompson, SG	39	4-9	1-5	0-0	0	2	2	2	0	1	0	0	9

BENCH	MIN	FGM-A	3PM-A	FTM-A	OREB	DREB	REB	AST	STL	BLK	TO	PF	PTS
David Lee, PF	15	3-7	0-0	3-6	0	5	5	3	0	0	0	1	9
James Michael McAdoo, SG	1	0-0	0-0	0-0	0	1	1	0	0	0	0	0	0
Andrew Bogut, C	3	0-0	0-0	0-0	0	1	1	1	0	0	1	3	0
Marreese Speights, C	2	0-2	0-0	1-2	1	1	2	0	0	0	0	1	1
Shaun Livingston, PG	25	2-4	0-0	3-4	1	7	8	4	1	1	1	3	7
Justin Holiday, SG	2	0-0	0-0	0-0	0	0	0	0	0	0	0	0	0
Leandro Barbosa, SG	7	1-3	0-1	0-0	0	0	0	1	0	0	0	1	2
Ognjen Kuzmic, C					DNP COACH'S DECISION								
Festus Ezeli, C					DNP COACH'S DECISION								
Brandon Rush, SG					DNP COACH'S DECISION								

TOTALS		FGM-A	3PM-A	FTM-A	OREB	DREB	REB	AST	STL	BLK	TO	PF	PTS
		36-77	12-30	19-27	6	38	44	24	5	5	7	21	103
		46.8%	40.0%	70.4%									

CAVALIERS

STARTERS	MIN	FGM-A	3PM-A	FTM-A	OREB	DREB	REB	AST	STL	BLK	TO	PF	PTS
LeBron James, SF	46	14-34	2-6	10-12	1	11	12	8	4	2	4	1	40
Timofey Mozgov, C	32	3-6	0-0	0-0	0	5	5	1	1	4	4	3	6
Tristan Thompson, C	44	4-6	0-0	2-4	4	9	13	1	0	0	1	1	10
Iman Shumpert, SG	32	1-2	1-2	0-2	0	3	3	0	3	0	2	4	3
Matthew Dellavedova, SG	39	7-17	2-6	4-5	1	4	5	4	0	0	2	3	20

BENCH	MIN	FGM-A	3PM-A	FTM-A	OREB	DREB	REB	AST	STL	BLK	TO	PF	PTS
James Jones, SF	18	0-3	0-1	0-0	0	3	3	0	0	1	1	1	0
Kendrick Perkins, C	3	0-2	0-0	2-2	0	1	1	0	0	0	0	1	2
Joe Harris, SG	3	0-0	0-0	1-2	0	0	0	0	0	0	0	0	1
Mike Miller, SG	3	0-0	0-0	0-0	0	0	0	0	0	0	0	0	0
J.R. Smith, SG	28	2-12	0-8	0-0	1	1	2	2	0	0	0	4	4
Brendan Haywood, C					DNP COACH'S DECISION								
Kyrie Irving, PG					DNP FRACTURED LEFT KNEECAP								
Shawn Marion, SG					DNP COACH'S DECISION								

TOTALS		FGM-A	3PM-A	FTM-A	OREB	DREB	REB	AST	STL	BLK	TO	PF	PTS
		29-88	4-27	20-28	16	33	49	16	2	3	9	19	82
		33.0%	14.8%	71.4%									

Flagrant Fouls: None
Technical Fouls: PLAYERS: None – TEAMS: None – COACHES: None
Officials: Joe Crawford, Mike Callahan, Ken Mauer
Attendance: 20,562
Time of Game: 2:37

Draymond Green added 17 points and Harrison Barnes had 14 for Golden State, which didn't lose three straight games all season while racking up 67 wins.

Since losing Game 3, the Warriors vowed to use the experience they gained when rallying from a 2-1 deficit against Memphis in the Western Conference semifinals.

"It's just a street fight," Green said. "Nobody's doing anything dirty, but they're battling and we're battling, and that's why this series is so exciting." ∎

WARRIORS 104 • CAVALIERS 91

CURRY LEADS WARRIORS TO BRINK OF NBA CHAMPIONSHIP

League MVP Stephen Curry made seven 3-pointers and scored 37 points, and the Warriors withstood another brilliant performance from LeBron James to outlast the Cleveland Cavaliers 104-91 for a 3-2 lead in the NBA Finals.

With a sellout crowd rocking and roaring in their golden-yellow shirts, Curry and his teammates took control of the game – and possibly the series – in the final minutes. Curry connected inside and out – sometimes way out – to help the Warriors pull away and get in a position they haven't been in 40 years.

The Warriors will try to win their first title since 1975 on Tuesday night in Cleveland, which hasn't won a major sports championship in 51 years.

"I feel confident because I'm the best player in the world," said James, who has carried Cleveland as much as he could.

The four-time MVP had 40 points, 14 rebounds and 11 assists, slowing down the pace the way only he can. He made 15 of 34 shots in 44 minutes.

"He has the ball in his hands a lot. Don't get discouraged if he makes shots. He's going to," Curry said of James. "Over the course of 48 minutes, we hope we wear him down to make it very tough on him."

Cleveland Cavaliers guard J.R. Smith (5) defends as Warriors' guard Stephen Curry (30) shoots. *AP Photo | Ben Margot*

Warriors' guard Stephen Curry, left, is guarded by Cleveland Cavaliers forward LeBron James.
AP Photo | Ben Margot

Draymond Green had 16 points and nine rebounds, Andre Iguodala added 14 points, eight rebounds and seven assists, and reserve Leandro Barbosa scored 13 points for the deep and talented Warriors.

Tristan Thompson tallied 19 points and 10 rebounds, and J.R. Smith scored all 14 of his points in the first half for Cleveland, which shot 39.5 percent and had no answer for Curry late.

"Not a lot you can do, honestly. He made some terrific shots," Cavs coach David Blatt said.

There were 20 lead changes and 10 ties in a game that featured nearly as many bruises as baskets – but few big men – and the league's two biggest attractions trading thrilling scores.

James made a 34-footer with the shot clock about to expire midway through the fourth to cut the Warriors' lead to 80-79. Curry answered with a step-back 3-pointer and Klay Thompson, who scored 12, followed with another.

Iguodala later hit a 3 and then grabbed a rebound, tossing in a left-handed putback while

Warriors' forward Harrison Barnes (40) dunks over Cleveland Cavaliers guard Mike Miller, left, and center Timofey Mozgov. *AP Photo | Ben Margot*

getting fouled by Tristan Thompson.

Curry added a cutting layup, then lost Dellavedova off the dribble and stepped back for a 3 that gave Golden State a 96-86 lead with 2:44 left.

James hit a 3-pointer, and the Cavs began fouling Iguodala -- a sub-par free throw shooter. But Curry never let the game get out of his hands, connecting on another 3-pointer with 1:12 remaining, sending fans into a frenzy and teammates running to give him hugs and high-fives.

"We didn't let the moment slip," Curry said.

James said the Cavs are content with the way they defended Curry.

"Was any of them not contested?" James said. "Falling, step-backs off the dribble. I'm OK with that. We're OK with that. You tip your hat to the best shooter in the league."

Kerr stuck with the small-ball lineup he used to help the Warriors win Game 4, starting swingman Iguodala over center Andrew Bogut. Blatt replaced 7-footer Timofey Mozgov with the streaky shooting Smith – sliding James to center – after Cleveland fell behind 8-2 in the opening minutes.

"I thought from the very beginning when they

Warriors' guard Klay Thompson (11) shoots over Cleveland Cavaliers guard Iman Shumpert (4).
AP Photo | Ben Margot

▲ **Warriors guard Stephen Curry (30) celebrates with fans.** *AP Photo | Eric Risberg*

▼ **Confetti falls at Oracle Arena after Game 5.** *AP Photo | Eric Risberg*

	1	2	3	4	T	Top Performers
Cleveland	22	28	17	24	91	Cle: L. James 40 Pts, 14 Reb, 11 Ast, 1 Stl
Golden State	22	29	22	31	104	GS: S. Curry 37 Pts, 7 Reb, 4 Ast, 2 Stl

CAVALIERS

STARTERS	MIN	FGM-A	3PM-A	FTM-A	OREB	DREB	REB	AST	STL	BLK	TO	PF	PTS
LeBron James, SF	45	15-34	3-8	7-9	1	13	14	11	1	0	2	5	40
Timofey Mozgov, C	9	0-1	0-0	0-0	0	0	0	0	1	0	2	2	0
Tristan Thompson, C	40	6-11	0-0	7-10	5	5	10	0	2	2	1	4	19
Iman Shumpert, SG	37	3-9	3-6	1-2	3	2	5	2	1	0	1	4	10
Matthew Dellavedova, SG	42	2-9	1-5	0-0	0	0	0	2	3	0	2	4	5

BENCH	MIN	FGM-A	3PM-A	FTM-A	OREB	DREB	REB	AST	STL	BLK	TO	PF	PTS
James Jones, SF	18	0-1	0-1	0-0	0	1	1	0	1	0	0	4	0
Mike Miller, SG	14	1-1	1-1	0-0	0	0	0	0	0	0	1	2	3
J.R. Smith, SG	36	5-15	4-14	0-0	1	6	7	2	1	2	1	3	14
Brendan Haywood, C		DNP COACH'S DECISION											
Kendrick Perkins, C		DNP COACH'S DECISION											
Kyrie Irving, PG		DNP KNEE INJURY											
Joe Harris, SG		DNP COACH'S DECISION											
Shawn Marion, SG		DNP COACH'S DECISION											

TOTALS		FGM-A	3PM-A	FTM-A	OREB	DREB	REB	AST	STL	BLK	TO	PF	PTS
		32-81	12-35	15-21	10	27	37	17	10	4	10	28	91
		39.5%	34.3%	71.4%									

WARRIORS

STARTERS	MIN	FGM-A	3PM-A	FTM-A	OREB	DREB	REB	AST	STL	BLK	TO	PF	PTS
Harrison Barnes, SF	29	3-7	0-0	2-4	6	4	10	2	2	1	1	3	8
Draymond Green, SF	36	4-9	1-3	7-10	0	9	9	6	0	1	4	4	16
Stephen Curry, PG	42	13-23	7-13	4-4	3	4	7	4	2	0	5	2	37
Andre Iquodala, SG	42	5-11	2-5	2-11	1	7	8	7	3	0	0	2	14
Klay Thompson, SG	40	5-14	1-4	1-1	0	3	3	2	0	0	1	5	12

BENCH	MIN	FGM-A	3PM-A	FTM-A	OREB	DREB	REB	AST	STL	BLK	TO	PF	PTS
David Lee, PF	9	1-3	0-0	0-0	0	1	1	1	0	0	1	2	2
Festus Ezeli, C	3	0-0	0-0	0-0	1	0	1	0	0	0	0	2	0
Shaun Livingston, PG	21	1-3	0-0	0-0	0	2	2	3	0	0	2	2	2
Leandro Barbosa, SG	17	4-5	1-1	4-4	0	2	2	0	0	0	2	3	13
James Michael McAdoo, SF		DNP COACH'S DECISION											
Andrew Bogut, C		DNP COACH'S DECISION											
Marreese Speights, C		DNP COACH'S DECISION											
Justin Holiday, SG		DNP COACH'S DECISION											

TOTALS		FGM-A	3PM-A	FTM-A	OREB	DREB	REB	AST	STL	BLK	TO	PF	PTS
		36-75	12-26	20-34	11	32	43	25	7	2	16	25	104
		48.0%	46.2%	58.8%									

Flagrant Fouls: 1 CLEVELAND (Smith 1)
Technical Fouls: PLAYERS: None – TEAMS: GOLDEN STATE (1) – COACHES: None
Officials: Jason Phillips, James Capers, Monty McCutchen
Attendance: 19,596
Time of Game: 2:39

went small, had their shooters out there, I thought this is Steph's night," Kerr said. "This is going to be a big one for him because he has all that room. He took over the game down the stretch and was fantastic."

Both teams lacked size. Neither lacked fight.

"We didn't turn it over, we were patient," Klay Thompson said. "And two words: Stephen Curry." ∎

WARRIORS 105 • CAVALIERS 97

GOLDEN STATE – NBA CHAMPIONS!

Their 40-year NBA championship drought is finally over. The Golden State Warriors once again reign supreme.

Stephen Curry and finals MVP Andre Iguodala scored 25 points apiece, Draymond Green recorded a triple-double and the Warriors – using a barrage of 3-pointers in the fourth quarter – won their first title since 1975 by finishing off LeBron James and the Cavaliers 105-97 on Tuesday night in Game 6.

After falling behind by two points early in the third quarter, the Warriors took control with Curry, the league's MVP, and Iguodala, who made his first start of the season in Game 4, leading the way.

"World champs," Curry said, letting the title sink in. "This is truly special. This group is a special group. From the time we started the season this is what we envisioned and a lot of hard work goes into it, all the way down to the last minute of this game. This is what it's all about. ... We're going to remember this for a long time."

Golden State allowed the Cavaliers to creep within eight points in the fourth before unleashing a flurry of 3s to ensure they would be taking the Larry O'Brien Trophy back to California. Curry's step-back made it 78-68, and after the

Warriors' guard Andre Iguodala (9) dunks against Cleveland Cavaliers forward James Jones (1). *AP Photo | Paul Sancya*

Warriors center Festus Ezeli (31) blocks the shot of Cleveland Cavaliers guard J.R. Smith (5) during the first half.
AP Photo | Tony Dejak

Cavs closed within seven on J.R. Smith's trey, Iguodala, Curry and Klay Thompson each drained one in a span of 81 seconds to make it 89-75.

Iguodala added another long shot for good measure before he strutted back on defense holding out three fingers on each hand.

James returned from Miami to deliver a title to his home region, but the 30-year-old, left to do most of the work by himself after All-Stars Kyrie Irving and Kevin Love were injured in the postseason, came two wins shy of giving Cleveland its first pro sports championship since 1964.

James had 32 points, 18 rebounds and nine assists in Game 6 and was dominant during the series, showing why he's the world's best player.

The Warriors were simply the better team.

James was replaced in the final seconds, but before he left the court, the four-time MVP shook hands with Curry and offered congratulations to head coach Steve Kerr and the rest of the Warriors.

"The sacrifice every guy made from Andre and David (Lee) stepping away from the starting lineup, we just played," Kerr said. "And they were all in it just to win. That's all that mattered. This is an amazing group of guys."

This series, which opened with two overtime games in Oakland, flipped when Kerr employed a small lineup in the fourth quarter of Game 3 and

The Golden State Warriors celebrate after wining Game 6 of basketball's NBA Finals against the Cleveland Cavaliers. *AP Photo | Darron Cummings*

Cleveland Cavaliers forward LeBron James (23) hugs Warriors' guard Stephen Curry (30) after the game. *AP Photo | Darron Cummings*

the Warriors nearly overcame a 20-point deficit before losing.

Kerr stuck with revamped lineup in Game 4, giving Iguodala a start, switching Green to center and benching the ineffective Andrew Bogut. The move was as golden as the Warriors, who finished with 83 wins, the third-highest single-season total in history.

Only the 1995-96 and 1996-97 Bulls won more, and Kerr was on both of those teams.

Cleveland fans did all they could to force a Game 7. The Warriors, though, were ready.

	1	2	3	4	T	Top Performers
Golden State	28	17	28	32	105	GS: S. Curry 25 Pts, 6 Reb, 8 Ast, 3 Stl
Cleveland	15	28	18	36	97	Cle: L. James 32 Pts, 18 Reb, 9 Ast, 2 Stl

WARRIORS

STARTERS	MIN	FGM-A	3PM-A	FTM-A	OREB	DREB	REB	AST	STL	BLK	TO	PF	PTS
Harrison Barnes, SF	35	3-8	3-4	0-0	0	2	2	2	1	0	0	3	9
Draymond Green, SF	41	6-13	2-5	2-4	1	10	11	10	3	1	3	5	16
Stephen Curry, PG	43	8-19	3-11	6-8	0	6	6	8	3	0	3	3	25
Andre Iquodala, SG	36	9-20	3-8	4-10	1	4	5	5	2	0	0	4	25
Klay Thompson, SG	25	2-7	1-3	0-0	0	5	5	2	0	1	2	6	5

BENCH	MIN	FGM-A	3PM-A	FTM-A	OREB	DREB	REB	AST	STL	BLK	TO	PF	PTS
David Lee, PF	1	0-1	0-0	0-0	0	0	0	0	0	0	0	0	0
Festus Ezeli, C	11	3-6	0-0	4-5	3	1	4	0	0	1	1	2	10
Shaun Livingston, PG	32	4-6	0-0	2-2	1	2	3	0	0	1	0	3	10
Leandro Barbosa, SG	15	2-5	1-3	0-0	1	2	3	1	2	0	0	1	5
James Michael McAdoo, SF					DNP COACH'S DECISION								
Andrew Bogut, C					DNP COACH'S DECISION								
Marreese Speights, C					DNP COACH'S DECISION								
Brandon Rush, SG					DNP COACH'S DECISION								

TOTALS		FGM-A	3PM-A	FTM-A	OREB	DREB	REB	AST	STL	BLK	TO	PF	PTS
		37-85	13-34	18-29	7	32	39	28	11	4	9	27	105
		43.5%	38.2%	62.1%									

CAVALIERS

STARTERS	MIN	FGM-A	3PM-A	FTM-A	OREB	DREB	REB	AST	STL	BLK	TO	PF	PTS
LeBron James, SF	47	13-33	2-10	4-8	3	15	18	9	2	0	6	3	32
Timofey Mozgov, C	33	5-8	0-0	7-8	7	5	12	2	0	4	3	3	17
Tristan Thompson, C	37	7-12	0-0	1-2	4	9	13	0	0	1	1	2	15
Iman Shumpert, SG	36	1-6	0-3	6-8	1	2	3	0	0	1	2	6	8
Matthew Dellavedova, SG	25	0-3	0-0	1-2	1	3	4	2	0	0	2	6	1

BENCH	MIN	FGM-A	3PM-A	FTM-A	OREB	DREB	REB	AST	STL	BLK	TO	PF	PTS
James Jones, SF	27	1-5	0-4	3-3	0	1	1	0	0	0	1	3	5
Joe Harris, SG	0	0-0	0-0	0-0	0	0	0	0	0	0	0	0	0
Mike Miller, SG	0	0-0	0-0	0-0	0	0	0	0	0	0	0	0	0
J.R. Smith, SG	34	5-15	4-9	5-8	0	5	5	1	1	1	1	3	19
Brendan Haywood, C					DNP COACH'S DECISION								
Kendrick Perkins, C					DNP COACH'S DECISION								
Kyrie Irving, PG					DNP FRACTURED LEFT KNEECAP								
Shawn Marion, SG					DNP COACH'S DECISION								

TOTALS		FGM-A	3PM-A	FTM-A	OREB	DREB	REB	AST	STL	BLK	TO	PF	PTS
		32-82	6-26	27-39	16	40	56	14	3	7	16	26	97
		39.0%	23.1%	69.2%									

Flagrant Fouls: None
Technical Fouls: PLAYERS: None – TEAMS: None – COACHES: None
Officials: Zach Zarba, Scott Foster, Marc Davis
Attendance: 20,562
Time of Game: 2:47

Down early after missing open shots, they began finding their range. Golden State capitalized on nine turnovers in the first quarter, made four 3s and built a 13-point lead when Harrison Barnes knocked down a long 3 – a shot that sent several dozen gold-and-blue Warriors fans sitting near their bench into a frenzy.

This was their night, the one they've waited for 40 years.■